The Joys
Of
Live Alchemy

by

Michael Levy

Point of Life, Inc.

ISBN 0-9668069-6-4.

Printed in the United States of America

Table of Contents

4

Poems by Michael Levy

Foreword

Every-thing in seamless form originates from no-thing. However, somewhere in the process of X-changes, from an empty void, to valid form, an awesome alchemical development takes place.
What is live alchemy or otherwise known as divine chemistry? Well, live alchemy is an intricate, fascinating, field of enchantment that contains many different multi dimensional projections in trans-formation. It has metaphysical, philosophical, scientific, religious, intellectual and intelligent meanings … All of them conjure-up changes in shape, size, color, texture, character, width, breadth, etc … from the observed human senses viewpoint …. Emerging from unknown sources … stopping for a short spell in mortal time…then traveling back into uncharted, timeless zones.

Human beings live on an earthly plane … however, there is a connection from heaven to earth that allows a mortal to change a dark negative into a beautiful colorful positive picture. Every cell, molecule, atom and particle in a human being is infused with divine chemistry that can change its construction. Within the human brain, live alchemy can change interpretations and meanings that will have an impact on a person's life in many ways

If a person neglects or misuses their alchemy's potential, their actions, or lack of, turn into random free radical acts that may have dire consequences. However, when they tune into the music of the enchantment within live alchemy, they live with good intent that produces a life overflowing with joyful feelings of divine bliss. That is the photo - genesis of true alchemy. It can blend religion with science, astrology with nature, invisible with witness, dust with humanity and all things in between. It channels universal intelligence into the realms of human logic and reason. The outcome from intelligent thought develops great discoveries, displayed on the worldwide stage, which aid humanity's daily actions and events.

Every-thing with form exists in a state of constant changing …Vast galaxies are spinning all around the universe, forming and reforming repeatedly. Infinite cosmic constructions continually change shape and size. Here on earth, the human body and mind are in constant change. Every cell, molecule and atom exists in a state of change. However, many people seem to stick with the same complex beliefs and biased perspectives throughout their lives, despite the heartache and suffering it brings.

On a personal level, some of the situations that can bring distress are; Stock market gyrations, death of a loved one, business cycles, divorce tribulations, illness symptoms, family disputes, financial worry; to name but a few. Consequently, you have been guided to read this book. Welcome into the living-light world of ... The Joys of Live Alchemy. Within these pages, you will find choices on which path to travel throughout your lifetime on earth. Each choice illuminates the mental strategies you can adopt and develop, to overcome the complexities of the human mind.

In a series of essays and short stories, you will discover alternatives to the way you now perhaps perceive your world to be. Each essay highlights the cause of ... depressive worry, debilitating anxiety, wealth deficiency, illness manifestation, emotional negativity and intellectual despondency.

Do not rush through each essay without taking the time to go over it a few times. You will find more meaning and different analysis each time you read each individual piece. Dissolving past negative memories takes time and patience. In uncovering your conditioned mind's views of life with all its assumptions, opinions, convictions, presumption and beliefs you will be able to determine if the choices you now retain are allowing you true freedom of alchemical thought.

Life can seem like an enigma of paradoxes if education and intellect are the only tools used to find the way through the mortal maze of modern day living. Humanity may try to make the truth fit into its variety of lifestyles. They can bend it, twist it ... misuse, and abuse it...but even God cannot change truth.

The identity you carry could be the cause of much sorrow and grief if you are not aware of the damage it can do to your health and wealth. A live alchemist can change negative situations into enlightening experiences... misrepresentations into facts....slants into equilibrium.....intellectual blindness into intelligent wisdom.... With the aid of live alchemy, every person can live a more genuine life on earth once the realization of the true self becomes a reality

A soul travels light and has no need of baggage. Thus, if you have no baggage to carry; there is no need of serious fixed labels to hinder your progress. If you understand you can continually change your inner recognition of mortal labels, you will not find life as such a laborious chore.

You are about to enter an alchemy zone of authentic meaning that will reveal the smooth, elegant and effortless path to valid, prosperous living. Enjoy cultivating your dependable seeds of life and observe how you leisurely blossom into a radiant live alchemist.

About the Cover Artist

CoverArt: Saleena Ki is a true living alchemist!
She is a StarSeed of de-lights whose extra-ordinary creations embody all Dimensions, Realms, Times, and Angles of Space. Her authentic mission is to activate change as a prolific Visionary Artist, Psychic-intuitive Transformation specialist, Meta-physician, Writer, Inventor, and Explorer, with numerous skills and deep understanding, which result in creative works. Her works have a deeply healing, activational, transformative effect on those who view them. She has a shamanic flair for gathering the newest vibrational colors that she retrieves from the universal infinite palette... Creating art that sparkles like colorful exquisite diamonds and gems, infused with lively glittering energy. She also weaves in living elements of life, love, light, fire, earth, air, water, sacred geometry, mathematical formulas, sounds, light codes and light languages. Her art seems to live, breath, and dance through the dimensions with a particular kind of vital aliveness. Designed to inspire, entice, activate, raise vibrations, invite and give permission to step fully into life and take it on with ecstatic joy and splendid power. Her artwork embodies and fuses Love, Joy and Power into one.

The art for the cover was created by merging one of her Art of Juicey Living® pieces with two Vibrakeys®: VK16, and VK34. VK34 was inspired by spending time with the whales and listening to their messages about using sacred geometry to assist and enhance alchemical living. The cover was created to visually express the pure joy of the added magic when we open heart-edly live alchemically.

She offers: Art: Alchemical Graphic Art, Commissioned Art, Sacred Custom Wall hangings, Soul Readings/Soul Portraits, Paintings and Murals that bring in transformational energies and open Stargates right in your home. Time and distance make no difference. We are all energy that can be read from anywhere. She offers life-changing support through her omni-dimensional use of Untangling (learned from Star Beings), Love, Light, Color, Sound, BodyTalk™, Physical and Lightbody Mechanics, Remote Viewing, Transformational Kundalini, The Vibrakeys®, StarSeed and StarKid Mediation.

Contact Info: Saleena Ki (aka Joan Ov"Art) lives in paradise on Maui, Hawaii 808-949-8720 toll free or email: saleena@vibrakeys.com
SpinningStarS free E-newsletter: Send Email to subscribe
Learn more about her work and art, or place orders visit:
The Vibrakeys® www.Vibrakeys.com
The Art of JuiceyLiving® www.TransformationalArt.com

About the Author

The words Live Alchemy are an anagram of Michael Levy. Therefore, in print and in life, Michael Levy is an authentic living alchemist.... Since there are no coincidences in life, it is appropriate that a true alchemist has a centered vision of change that includes...
Foresight and insight, ying and yang, cause & effect, eternity and temporal, nature and nurture, mystic and thinker, light and dark, air and water, fire and earth, intellect and intelligence, balance and slant, academia & wisdom

In the temporal world, he has turned poverty into wealth, weak genes into strong healthy genes and happiness into divine bliss. Health, wealth and joy are the three blessings that Michael represents and he would like to share them with you.

Michael was born in Manchester, England on the 6th March 1945. At the tender age of nineteen, he started his own textile company with just a few pounds. The business continued to grow into a well-established and successful wholesale textile company for over thirty years. Michael also owned and managed large commercial buildings in the city center, Manchester.

He has invested in the stock market successfully for over forty years and dealt in all types of commodities. His simple methods of investing bring enough rewards but not excessive amounts.
After many life experiences and a successful, joy-filled business career, he retired to Florida in 1992.

It took six years of deep thought and inner questions, pondering the meaning of life, before Michael could express his intuitive values and significant worth.

In 1998 Michael established Point of Life, Inc., as a vehicle to project his alchemy philosophy and spiritual understanding. The Point of Life website and the associated newsletter (Point Of Life Global Newsletter) are freely accessible by anyone who has access to a computer. Michael is a fluent speaker on radio and television. He was a host on Voice America.com radio for a short time. He is available for seminars and meetings to share and discusses his views about the purpose of life, finding the peace and enjoyment that lead to a healthy, stress-free life.

In 2002, Michael received an invitation to become a member of the prestigious Templeton Speaker's Bureau... A short time later, the bureau disappeared into empty space. Occasionally he can be located on cruise ships, laughing and joking whilst giving life enhancement lectures. He is an unusual poet, alchemy philosopher and uncommon author, who writes from the heart and soul... His four inspirational books challenge normal, conventional style.

"What is the Point?" - "Minds of Blue Souls of Gold"- "Enjoy Yourself - It's Later Than You Think" and "Invest with a Genius."

When the words "Inspirational books" are typed into a Google search engine, Michael's website ranking is number one, out of many inspirational web sites.

Michael's poetry and essays now grace many web sites, journals and magazines throughout the world. His philosophies contain relative alchemy in Truth, Wisdom and Love that are out of the reach of most educated people at this moment in time. However, change is in emergence ... Just one example from many... The Royal Collage of Psychiatry over the past two years has published five of his works in their spiritually themed newsletter.

"If you spend all your life laughing and joking you will have no time for a serious illness."

Live Alchemy
I am thankful for ... all the best awards, I will never obtain,
and delight in, the only one that really counts,
I would like to thank all the distinguished, powerful people, who;
Almost nominated me for ... the Nobel peace prize, but never did,
Almost nominated me for ... the Pulitzer Prize, but never did,
Almost nominated me for ... prime minister of England, but never did,
Almost nominated me for ... king of England, but never did,
Almost nominated me for ... president of the USA, but never did,
Almost nominated me for ... ruler of the world, but never did,
Almost nominated me for ... ruler of the universe, but never did,
However, more than any nomination,
could ever bring... is heartfelt appreciation,
for being bestowed ... with the award of birth,
living on earth's, delectable paradise as,
a mortal-being, who is given the opportunity,
to savor the joy of each second on earth.

Opening Orchestration

Everything is Relative

Everything relates to nothing ... Nothing is relative to everything. When you live as nothing you have no-thing to lose and can turn into any-thing you wish.

Living life in an ever-changing universe can become complex and distressing for most human beings. Everything on earth has a connection to everything else if we take the time to search for their origin. Albert Einstein's theory of relativity changed the whole complexion of humanity's tone, hue and texture. From a personal human point of view, all things are relative to the perceiver of the thought of the moment. Einstein once stated, "If you put your hand on a hot stove for a minute it will seem like an hour. If you sit with a pretty girl for an hour, it will seem like a minute."

If humanity can find reasons why it continually seems to be uneasy with its developments, perhaps it can learn to live a more authentic existence.
Why do people... Die too young?
Why do people... Never have enough money?
Why do people... Always seem to find something that makes them unhappy?
Why do people... Develop a debilitating illness?
Why do people... Keep seeing the grass greener on the other side of the fence?
Why do people... Find conflict with other people beliefs?
Why do people... Cultivate addictive harmful habits?
Why do people... Embrace negative emotions?
Why do people... Follow the herd, even when they sense it is the wrong thing to do?
Why do people... Fight wars when they recognize there are no winners, just some lose less?

The answers to these questions and an infinite number of other questions are established once we detect the relative cause and effect of everything that stems from nothing. This may seem a little obscure, but as we dissect each event and action we encounter, we locate authentic meaning, once we become a living alchemist.
For instance, many golfing equations need an answer before a golfer can become a scratch player. Even when they become a professional and can

go around the course in par, you might thing their problems are over…No; they just begin anew with a completely fresh batch of troubling issues.

Every golfer should be aware that, a wrong thought, or ineffective body movement precedes every bad shot. So, what causes erroneous thought? Many answers go begging for consequential questions. Here are a few.

Was it emotional negativity?
Was it a lack of judgment?
Was it an outside distraction?
Was it just by chance?
What was the cause of the ineffective body movement?
Was it a lack of practice?
Was it a technical habitual fault?
Was it a physical injury?
Was it food not digested properly?
Was it constipation?
Was it a sudden pain?

The questions asked apply to every person in every walk-of-life, not just golf. The answers to all the questions emanate from a chain of events that leads up to each miss-hit shot or lost opportunity. There is an element of luck referred to as rub of the green in every game of life. There is also the random element such as a sudden blast of stormy weather. However, when the mortal being become a live alchemist, it turns a potential bad outcome of happenings into a winning game of life, because the authentic source of wisdom, guides the life-player and the ego steps aside and lets it happen. Every golfer is aware that the game of golf is a good reflection in the game of life. It has its ups-and-downs, and in the end, you're left with a scorecard to tally up your triumphs and failures.
When your time on earth is over, how will you mark your card? Will it be overflowing with bogus, negative beliefs that lead you to an early demise … or … Will it take you to the fairway of thought that projects a prosperous lived existence?

Here are a few more questions that need authentic answers and like golf, only you can tot up your score, for it only applies to you and your maker and is nobody else's concern.
Mark your own card and just answer Yes or No

Do you smoke?
Do you drink more than two glasses of alcohol each month?
Do you enjoy sex?

Are you more than ten pounds overweight?

Do you worry or feel anxious more than a couple of times a week?

Are you in a happy state of mind more than ninety percent of the time?

Do you believe in God, if so, how does your belief affect your life?

Is your faith more important than your joy?

Do you blame the Jews for the death of Christ?

Would you be happy if your son or daughter married a person with a different skin color?

Do you have a pet hate or does other people's habits ever annoy you?

Can you sit in complete silence, with a totally empty mind, for more than fifteen minutes?

Do you love yourself?

Do you have enough money?

Do you enjoy your work?

Do you love animals?

Do you eat red meat more than twice a week?

Are you successful?

Do you ever get sick i.e.... Hold symptoms more than two days?

Do you walk, swim or exercise for more than twenty minutes, four times a week?

Do you have any addictions?

Do you really know who you are?

When you have calculated your score, put it in a safe place... Then after you read this book, tot it up again and see if it is the same score. You will have a much clearer picture on what you need to bring about, so that you can delight in your reality, in a comfortable enchantment zone that is older than time itself.

Part One - Prelude to Wealth Alchemy

The Five Alchemy Principles for Prosperity

Forty years ago, I started my first business at the tender age of nineteen. The street markets in and around Manchester, England were my happy hunting ground. Every day was an adventure, and despite the weather and difficulties of getting a stall on the street market, life was always fun and enjoyable. There was always some comical incident, even when I had to stand in the pouring rain, with no customers in sight. Moreover, if there was no amusing event to focus on, I created one and made other people laugh.

"Never continue in a job you don't enjoy. If you're happy in what you're doing, you'll like yourself, you'll have inner peace. And if you have that, along with physical health, you will have had more success than you could possibly have imagined." - Johnny Carson

Within a few years, the alchemy magic began to bear fruit. I opened a wholesale textile company. I went on to become a very successful businessperson, not only making money in my original business but also in commercial property and the stock market. I retired from the business world at forty-six years of age.

After a six-year time-out period, so that I could understand why I was successful with no effort, the alchemy magic produced remarkable results. I reinvented myself and became…an author, poet, philosopher, motivational/inspirational/financial speaker, radio show host, director, producer and many other labels. How was it possible to achieve so much, without a mention of the word "work" in my vocabulary? Well, you see, I just enjoy everything I do; if it is enjoyable, how can I class it as work? I just let nature take its course and leave the outcome in the hands of the master alchemist. I understand everything happens at the appropriate moment for the fitting reasons.

"Every now and then go away, have a little relaxation, for when you come back to your work your judgment will be surer. Go some distance away because then the work appears smaller and more of it can be taken in at a glance and a lack of harmony and proportion is more readily seen." - Leonardo Da Vinci
When I read the headlines in the newspapers describing the corruption and scandals in large and small corporations I wonder why the executives had

to lie and cheat to earn money? It is far easier and less risky to make money the honest way, so why do people do things the hard way and end up in disgrace?

• What makes some people believe they need a billion dollars to be happy?
• Why has greed become so fashionable?
• Why in many instances do we seem to treat our fellow human worse than a wild dog?

"The brain is a wonderful organ; it starts working the moment you get up in the morning, and does not stop until you get into the office." - Robert Frost

Our animal instincts, although contained in a civilized package, can be savage and uncaring, especially in the business world. It has become dog-eat-dog.

As we climb the ladder of success there are many other folks on higher rungs who may try to kick us down. There are also those who have not got on the first rung yet who will try and pull us down. So how do we cope in a modern day world of hungry hounds, eager to get their hands on as much money as possible any way they can?

"Being busy does not always mean real work. The object of all work is production or accomplishment and to either of these ends there must be forethought, system, planning, intelligence, and honest purpose, as well as perspiration. Seeming to do is not doing." - Thomas Alva Edison

In life, there is always an easy way and a hard way to do everything, so how about I share with you five simple alchemy principles of business that cannot fail?

Principle Number One: Enjoy everything.
We should understand the world does not owe us a living. We will succeed or fail by the amount of joy we have for the project we will call our work. The number one ingredient is enthusiasm and commitment for the job in hand.

We have to understand that very few things will go in the direction we desire, and the more we practice our skills, the luckier we will become. We manufacture our own luck, and recognizing opportunities is the key to success.

Every viewpoint, in every business day, ought to be explored. Never say no to anything until we have examined every possibility and outcome. Even if we find that it is not what we desire, we leave the door open for future development. If we are only interested in what we can get out of any action of the moment, we are doomed to failure.

Principle Number Two: Become a giver not a taker.
A key ingredient in a successful venture is giving rather than taking. In other words give the best and you will receive the best. If you do not have the ability to give the best, keep on trying different approaches until you can give the best. Whatever you give, you will get back in abundance. The mistake many people make is they want to take as much as they can, as quick as they can, with the least amount of giving.

There are those who have achieved money and status by devious means. They may have all the trappings of the luxury lifestyle, but they do not possess the clear mind to enjoy the fruits of their labor. Therefore, they are not a success to themselves.

All the stresses and strains of cheating will one-day manifest into an illness. You can mislead other people, but you cannot lie to your immune system. Therefore, it pays big dividends to give other associates a helping hand up the ladder of success. Alchemy works in both directions so if you oppose the good ... you will end up with the bad.

Principle Number 3: Overcome adversity.
Enjoy the failures more than the successes. Understand, there is no such thing as failure. Each lesson learnt, is a lesson gained. Just don't keep making the same mistakes. Everything is a gain, gain situation. Negative people are our stepping-stones to wealth. The more they tell us it can't be done, the more energy they give us to get the job done successfully. Always remember, beauty is relative to the eye of the beast. Adversities are sent to test our resolve ... become a good hurdler, and learn how to jump over them.

If you require an answer to a difficult problem you need to solve, ask any question to yourself a few minutes before going to sleep—and then forget about it and go into a sound deep sleep. The next morning, on awakening, you may get an idea from "out-of-the-blue" that solves the issue. If not that morning, then it may take more time. Keep asking the question every night until the matter resolves itself...if it is a genuine question then you surely will find a truthful answer! If, after a long period, you cannot find any answers that solve your predicament, then examine the question. Distinguish if it is to serve the greater good of your business and everyone connected with it, or just a selfish search for instant wealth. Change the question and you will find the authentic answer. Then perhaps you can change your attitude to the problem.

Principle Number Four: Stay debt-free.
Not too many people became millionaires by being in personal or business debt and paying high interest rate charges. Why put yourself behind the field before you start the race?
It is far better to walk before you can run. You must not pile up too much debt. If you cannot afford something, then you need to work a little harder and longer until you have the funds to expend. I know this is not the modern way of thinking and there are always exceptions to the rule, but being debt-free sure makes for 'peaceful sleep.' Being 'under pressure' to pay bills is no way to live. So practice, plastic surgery and cut up most of your credit cards. Your purpose of being on earth is to enjoy life and your labor must be a labor of love without demands. The greater the love for the job -in -hand ... the more rewarding the prosperity results.

Principle Number Five: Enjoy endurance.
Remember the three P's Patience, Persistence, and Perseverance. If we trust in our 'true self,' we cannot fail. As long as we are enjoying our business activities in the same way as we enjoy our leisure, success is assured. If it takes a few years more than we thought to achieve our goal, then so much the better, because we have more time to gain extra experience.

Personal integrity cannot be bought; therefore, once we gain authentic credibility, everything else we do eases into its appropriate space. It will eventually mean other people will regard us as experts in our field. We have mastered time and space.

With these five principles for prosperity deposited into our memory banks, we are ready to build new bridges, network with all the new and innovative companies in our field.

"I still need more healthy rest in order to work at my best. My health is the main capital I have and I want to administer it intelligently." - Ernest Hemingway

There is just one other point to understand. It is important to note that we will never actually own anything. We only possess what we can take on our eternal journey. We are just renting space and time, so our success, is not measured by our bank balance. We live in a materialistic world, and to become truly prosperous we need to establish one very important point ... When we reverse our conditioned mind's way of thinking, we find creativity within a universal spirit, guiding us on an authentic life course ... Intelligence is channeled from the spirit with-in ... Are you connected-in-frequently? When the frequency is tuned-in to the authentic wave bands, we incorporate powerful-foundation-seeds ... Yielding an easy direction to follow towards alchemical prosperity!

Alchemy haiku

Mind-full duality
Differ rant n rave
Just another angle

In the yardage book
sizing up life
from here to eternity

Never-ending paradise
home from home
built on a whim

Too much source
many geese
flocks of karma

Sunday morning assembly
filled with spirit
at O'Really's pub

In the great hall
many great people meet
grating on each others nerves

A-we-so-me
won-der-men-tally
car-e-free?

Eternal Triumph of Joy

There is an ancient Greek tale of a man named Sisyphus. He was a playful trickster who played his pranks on everyone, including the gods. One day he fooled the god of death and locked him in a cupboard. Of course, the death god was not too pleased and when the other gods eventually released him, he condemned Sisyphus to an eternity of rolling a large, heavy boulder up a mountain. When he reached the top, the boulder would not rest and it rolled all the way down the mountainside to the bottom. This then was his eternal tormented load to bear, or so it would seem.

However, there is another way of looking at this story. Once Sisyphus got to the top he had a long time to enjoy himself as he made his way back down to the bottom. He would have a great view on the mountaintop and could savor all the magnificent scenery and wild flowers on the way down. When he started his task repeatedly, he could think what a great workout he's been given and how it will help him keep fit and healthy. He could break out into song and sing... `Oh! What a beautiful morning,' ...as he takes his deep breaths, whilst gritting his teeth to push the rock up to the summit.

He could observe the beauty in each vein of the rock and feel its sensational texture. He would have all the time in the outer-world to understand the rock and he are one and the same. He could instruct his mind to believe the rock was actually pulling him up the mountain and it was he, who was resisting the rocks power. He could play a game of push and pull. He could be thankful for the great strength the gods had given him so he is able to continue his labor of love and fun. He could blow them kisses and make up jokes for them, so that their mockery and laughter will focus on the jokes... which may be, forever, on them.

We all have our rocks to push up mountains. Whether it is our stock market portfolio boulder that seems to be rising nicely.... then crash...it is at the bottom again. Perhaps a person becomes a writer, artist, teacher or shop assistant, etc, and feels life is unfair... that other people are not grateful for their contributions and efforts they continue to roll out.

Maybe mothers and fathers feel their children are not thankful for all their loving kindness and visa versa from the children's perspective. So many situations in life where a person feels as though they are given seemingly hard tasks to perform...they consider their lot in life is not a happy one... It only comprises of more and more hard toil, ridicule, complains and mockery as their rewards.

If we turn the tables on the way we view our efforts and enjoy our tasks no matter how taxing and difficult they appear to be, we may find they are not that demanding and formidable at all. The secret lies in not letting other people or false gods, take away our joy of living, no matter what labors we have to implement. I think you get the gist... Therefore, here is your question to
Ponder ... When your life on earth is nearing its end and you look back on each event, do you want it to be recorded as A Tale of Woe or A Story of Joy......Always remember....
It is your rock...your mountain... and your freedom of thought can make all the difference.

From the glow of enthusiasm, I let the melody escape. I pursue it. Breathless I catch up with it. It flies again, it disappears, it plunges into a chaos of diverse emotions. I catch it again, I seize it, I embrace it with delight... I multiply it by modulations, and at last I triumph in the first theme. There is the whole symphony." - Beethoven.

"Every great and commanding moment in the annals of the world is the triumph of some enthusiasm". - Ralph Waldo Emerson.
"Joy in looking and comprehending is nature's most beautiful gift".
- Albert Einstein

The Wisdom of the Dead

Dead people are
the most intelligent people
not on earth
for they now know
the truth
and realize what
put them
in their graves
If only un-dead people
would awaken
to fathom
the wisdom of the dead.

Truthful Investment Savvy

A Philosophy for the Individual Investor
Generating substantial amounts of money from the stock and commodity markets takes a special flair. Both markets occasionally act in random chaotic movements, within set trading ranges, or trends for given moments in time. Withstanding chaotic moments is essential for survival in the investment jungle. Losing a few short-term battles must be mentally acceptable in winning the long-term gains.

Sooner-or-later, all trends change and if the investor/ trader does not change with them, they will forfeit their money. In the stock market, conceivably it may be later. In the commodity markets, the losses are more likely to be a lot sooner.

The biggest handicap a person exhibits is the delusion established by their own personal opinions on which direction, they rigidly believe, any financial market or particular stock will journey. People talk about being bullish or bearish and become very adamant about the direction they believe their interests will travel. Being stuck in any cemented mind-set is a sure way to ruin.

The biggest curse could be a "good education," for the more a person supposedly knows about investments and trades, the more likely it becomes that they will fix their attitude and opinions to establish camp as a bull or a bear. Education should be employed as a tool for interpreting and relaying information. It should not be used as a medium of setting the mind in stone.

In today's world, there are multitudes of trading systems, which can assist the investor/ trader. Gathering all the information the hi-tech world provides should be a good thing...So, if it is "a good thing"... why doesn't every financially educated person make money? All the information they collect and compile is, in all likelihood, the reason why they do not make money. It is not
that the information is faulty... It is the manner in which it is envisioned and interpreted that has shortcomings.

Circumstances change, and what started out as a good tip or idea can become a losing proposition for a myriad of reasons. So how can a regular person who wants to get rich, earn money in financial markets, without dependence on "experts or gurus," who rarely make substantial money for their clients, over a long period. Well, the individual investor needs to become a compass with no fixed direction... A barometer with - no high or low.

Visualize a dial that has north-east-south-west on it. The investor is a human arrow that is unrestrained and is free to move in any direction. However, desire and opinion is removed from the make up of the human arrow. There is no glass to cover the dial and the arrow will travel in the direction the wind blows. The arrow has no independent choices to ponder ... It must move with the winds direction, no matter how it has been assembled. If it resists the wind's power, it will divorce from its dial and will elude true direction. (Go Broke!)

The arrow's direction moves by an intelligence magnetism that is beyond its grasp, yet it is in reach of its awareness, therefore it can be mobilized in any fashion. What this means is; the human mind is susceptible to change from a force it does not recognize, yet it knows it exists in an intangible manner, which is comparable to the wind. This compelling magnetism breeds ... Truthful Investment Savvy. The investor empowerment policy becomes ... Truthful Investment Savvy.

Once the investor/ trader release their obstructed mind-set convictions, and they enhance an open observational approach to every transaction, they will have a greater chance to earn money in the markets. It does not mean they will not slip back into old traits and make mistakes. The acknowledgement of the mistakes is a litmus test, which explains how the actions went against the direction of the wind (market forces). Instead of relying on opinions formulated from sources that may or may not be true, they position their minds awareness to become a ...
Proactive transformation energy.

  - Information is identified, correlated, and then linked to ways it will move in synchronicity with a market or stock, without a personal opinion hindrance.

  - Instead of reacting with fear or greed to information, they move with grace and harmony into each deal.

  - They are not afraid to take a profit or loss.
  - They may lose many battles but they know they will win the war.

- Setbacks and adversities become a power fuel that infuses the energy, to re-consign any loss into an increased profit at a later date.
- They entrust their financial future to no other human being.
- They command their own ship with benevolence and kindness to other people.

- They find there decision-making skills continue to expand and relate to greater profits.

- Restrictions of attitude and opinions fade away and reside in a quite corner of the mind.

-    Stubborn pride and unyielding presumptions give way to the authentic reason for being in the market... It is to make money, not to defend the Ego. ... Buying a stock is a date, not a marriage.

A new financial warrior is born who enjoys every transaction no matter the outcome.

The game; 'TIS afoot and open to infinite possibilities,
'TIS the adrenaline of pure potential, flowing through the veins,
The blood; 'TIS transfused with universal intelligence,
   it flows into every cell and molecule of the mind/body.

Now the investor/ trader can go forth and multiply with Truthful Investment Savvy.

What's in a Name?
The Stock Exchange,
Straddled with Bulls, Bears and Stags,
A faux farmhouse,
Mask the... pen and ink!
Time and money to invest,
What's the option?
Perhaps a change of name..........
The Rascal House?
Call; for a pastrami-on-rye
Put; on plenty of ketchup and mustard
Order; executed and full-filled.

The Excellent Writer Within

The art of good writing comes from the artist within. All humans have the ability to become great authors, poets, artists and musicians, etc., so why do most folks find it such a difficult task? Why do many people say I could never be a writer or I could never aspire to write poetry? Moreover, why do folks who do write grow discouraged when their work is rejected?

We are what we think, so if we believe we cannot succeed in our daily actions, then for sure we will never get away from our perception of what we think we are. This self-defeating attitude was not of our making. As we were growing up and maturing into adulthood, we were indoctrinated with thousands of negative thoughts. This gave us a belief that we are only homemakers or only truck drivers. This limited vision of our role in life gives us a limited life. People the world over have great creativity. Once we start to understand who we are and the reasons we exist, we start to cultivate eloquent works of creativity.

Just writing worthy, meaningful, literature will not get the success it deserves unless we possess the resolve to carry on writing in spite of the critics. There will always be those who criticize a writer, no matter how well the composition. Rejection is an everyday experience for most writers. This is a joy we must accept and grow from. Just because someone does not like our essay does not mean it has no value. It means it was not acceptable to the editor or book reviewer who was reading the essay.

We can do two things when we feel constant rejections. We can give up and say, it was not meant to be. Alternatively, we can say, "How do I become a better writer and have my work accepted by more of the establishment?'" Once a small section of the general public starts to take an interest in our writing, the sheep mentality of the "establishment" will no doubt follow. It always has. It always will. Success breeds success.

Until we can find the inner core of creativity and start to write from the soul, we will never become great writers. We may achieve a modicum of success by writing a few columns for a newspaper or magazine but that could keep us in a vacuum. We can scrape a living, but may not amass a fortune, for we are trying to write and trying will never cut the mustard.

The secret to excellent writing is to enjoy with ecstatic abandonment each letter and syllable we put down on paper. The pure joy of writing makes us successes; nothing else will. Those who tell us we have to struggle and sweat have not grasped true meaning in their lives. We need no approval of any human to be a success.

Stop trying to become a success. We are successes already. We were born. We are the success of life. The sperm hit the egg and here we are...
Hello world!
Everything else we do and achieve is just a bonus.

Life is to be enjoyed, not endured. Joy brings true meaning to life.
Now the next question to ask is "what is joy?" What does joy mean and how do we achieve it? Look within , take time to silence the mind and feel the texture of nothingness. Smell the perfume of celestial splendor. Discover the sound of cosmic waves flowing though your subconscious mind. Palpate infinity. Breathe eternity. Conceive the splendor of maturating into the essence of a successful writer. Be the word, become the poem, and live the adventure. Everything we do is inscribed in our soul's book of life. We just need to learn how to read the instructions written within every cell and molecule of our being.
Each tissue and sinew bleeds muscular power of infinite, majestic might. Fly on the wings of limitless mastery. Escape the shrouded cocoon and become the enchanting butterfly. The dreams of authentic reality are about to manifest a rainbow of magical delights:_____
"Write on Time" _____ "Compose in Space"
J_ust
O_bey
Y_ourself ___ (THE GENIUS)

His Milestone

He worked hard, for Twenty-five years,
His business was a huge success,
The biggest in town,
A new milestone,
Hitting the headlines, in all the local newspapers,
Quite an achievement, since he started out with nothing,
He made a speech, saying he would retire soon,
Low and behold, new, more venturesome firms abounded,
Competition grew fierce,
No problem; he was up to the task,
After fifty years in the business, he was the biggest in the country,
A new milestone
Catching the headlines, in all the national newspapers,
He gave a speech,
Saying he would definitely retire, very shortly,
However new, novel, unfamiliar competition snowballed,
Nevertheless, he was up to the task,
After sixty-five years in business, he was the biggest in the world,
A new milestone,
Striking the headlines, in every newspaper in the world,
That day as he prepared, to make his speech to retire...
His milestone, became his headstone.

Ten Alchemy Tidings for Authentic Living

The pressures of living in the twenty-first century have greatly expanded. In fact, as each year passes by, more and more stress and tensions appears to build up in the majority of people's lives. One factor that brings misery and suffering is the thought that we are responsible for other people's actions and thoughts. For instance, it is normal for a father and mother to take responsibility for their family's welfare.

They need to be good husbands and wives to each other and provide money for the family's food and shelter. They also require being a mentor for the children, and guiding them on a true path of life. If they work for a company, they need to take responsibility for the company's progress in their respective department or area of expertise. Then they have friends, relations and other acquaintances who may call on them for help and advice. A whole mountain of responsibilities, right? ... No - absolutely wrong!

S/he has only one responsibility the whole of his/her life on earth, and it is only to him or her self.

Yes, that is right...only to him or her self. Do you assume that it is selfish statement to make? Only to take responsibility for one's own actions and not those of others.... Well, just hold on for a moment before you jump the gun.

People on earth can only be responsible for themselves and what I mean by that is:

Each person encompasses, within himself or herself, a response-ability, to keep balanced and centered at all times. Every individual needs to have the ability-to-respond to each-and-every eventuality they face in their lifetime with wisdom and fortitude. Sometimes it may mean doing things in an unorthodox manner.

I remember a funny story about a Rabbi who went from town to town, delivering the same sermon every time. His driver was being bored and asked if the Rabbi could deliver a new sermon at the next town. The rabbi had a better idea. Since they had never been to the town before, nobody knew who the rabbi was. Moreover, because the driver knew the sermon backwards he would let him deliver it and the rabbi would sit at the back of the room.

All went well and the driver conveyed a magnificent sermon, word for word. However, a very learned professor of theology stood up and asked him about a problem he has with chapter five, verse ten in Genesis and would the rabbi please explain it to him. The speaker thought for a moment and replied; "Why, that is so simple... I will let my driver answer you."

All human beings need to possess the response ability to know how to keep themselves healthy, wealthy and happy, no matter what negative forces try to knock them off course. When disasters strike, they need to know how to regroup their resources and use them in the way nature intended. In other words, to use their natural organic brain-power, to its full potential. Moreover, the reason they need to be able to personally respond wisely to each event that comes their way is....

If they cannot take charge of their own actions, behavior, demeanor, resilience, courage, fearlessness, kindness and grace etc...Why then, they certainly cannot take responsibility for even looking after the cat. Sooner-or-later, both the cat and its 'responsible' keeper are going to be crying over spilt milk. For if, a man or a woman cannot control their own emotions and belief systems in an authentic manner, they will only make matters worse for the people they love the most. Eventually they will make themselves sick.

If they allow their taste buds to dictate to the rest of the body what foods it should eat, without understand what the bodies' digestive and immune system desires, they will become unhealthy human beings.

If they allow outdated belief systems, derived from mythology, that contain fear and revenge, to guide their path, then they will live a miserable life and make everyone they come into contact with miserable also.

Every human being is very well equipped, with a super-sonic brain-wave-band-system that can charge up his or her intelligent energy so that it provides every requirement to live a prosperous life on earth. Once they are tuned into the correct channels of infinite wisdom and knowledge they can then, and only then, help others to locate their own inner genius....And that my friends is Your Response Ability.....And no-one else's. You see

your pact, bond and linkage is with God and no one else. Always
remember the Ten Tidings for authentic living...

1 ... One ounce of compassion is worth more than the advice of a
million lawyers.

2 ... One glass of water is worth more than an ocean of champagne.

3 ... One kind word is worth more that a ten new Rolls Royce's.

4 ... One minute of silence is worth more than a lifetime of idle chatter.

5 ... One agreement is worth more than a thousand wars, for everyone
loses in a war, no matter what the outcome.

6 ... One act of love is worth more than a royal crown

7... One tear of laugh is worth more than a mansion filled with tears of
sorrow

8 ... One joyful thought is worth more than a hospital full of medicine

9 ... One moment of divine bliss is worth more than a billion dollars

10 ... One lifetime of true joy is worth more than an eternity of
mediocrity.

On reflection, there is only One source of true bliss and well-being
and when you follow it, you walk a true path and are one of the few
who posses Response Ability... The ability-to-respond to spirit's,
pure, virtuous intent.

The Sun Shines on the Righteous

The sun shines, through the window,
ancient dust can be seen,
drifting, into every crevice,
 in your opulent, luxurious room,
they coat the old master paintings,
valued in millions,
who are these, timeworn inhabits,
who now float, around your room,
in clandestine powder,
invisible by lamp light,
intangible, in microscopic garb,
what dramas, do they select, that, relates to you,
can you attend, their silent laughter,
grasp their muted tears,
organic dust, floating, on beams of sunlight,
time to call in the cleaners perhaps,
spring clean them away,
suck them into a vacuum,
but, in your heart, you admit,
you can never cleanse them from your soul.

How to Gain from Negatively Slanted News

Sometimes the stock market goes on a roller coaster ride when there is no clear vision of what the future holds in store. Every year there is a low point when the indices trade at their yearly lows for no real reason apart from sensationalistic panic that has no truthful foundation. That is a good point of enter for stock you have on your, "to buy" wish list

"How many legs does a dog have if you call the tail a leg? Four; calling a tail a leg doesn't make it a leg." - Abraham Lincoln.

Any person who is looking for common sense will not find much in the gyrations of the stock market when there is high volatility. In today's media world, unfounded fears and negatively slanted opinions, feeds the public. The naive TV commentators and over-reactive newspaper editors supply the erroneous nutriments.

"Believe nothing just because a so-called wise person said it. Believe nothing just because a belief is generally held. Believe nothing just because it is said in ancient books. Believe nothing just because it is said to be of divine origin. Believe nothing just because someone else believes it. Believe only what you yourself test and judge to be true."
- Buddha.

When one set of government statistics are released, the doom and gloom merchants jump on the bandwagon to spout their well-chosen words and hey presto ... The markets go down.

A typical comment will be "The next six months company results will be poor because the latest figures indicate the economy is getting weaker." How can they possibly know what the company results will be in six months time?

"All truths are easy to understand once they are discovered; the point is to discover them." - Galileo.

A few days later, another bunch of controlling experts will come on TV and declare; "The economy is too strong and interest rates will have to rise steeply ... so the next six months company results will be weak ... Everyone should sell their shares and get out of the markets ASAP." How can they conceivably discern what events establish themselves in six months time?

What happened to honest reporting ... that just disclosed the facts?

The only people who stand to strike short term gain, in the stock markets uncalled for downturn, are the ones with billions of dollars in hedge fund short positions ... It is they who raise their cups of plenty and sing... Three cheers for, negatively slanted financial news ... reported by mislead comment-taters. However, long-term, very few people earn money by shorting stocks.

"Where large sums of money are concerned, it is advisable to trust nobody." - Agatha Christie.

People with common sense will always make intelligent interpretations and in the long run come out on top ... The smart investor buys cheaply, the companies that negatively slanted reports may try and distort. They know a company with strong, honest balance sheets, mindful management, sound products and serving the public with what they desire, will make them money.

"Love all, trust a few." - William Shakespeare

The astute investors will buy when others are selling out of fear ... In the long run that is how millionaires are made. Let the Wall Street fiddlers play the tunes for a while and maybe the media fools will dance in rhythmic ignorance... However, in the end, the wise investor will reap the rewards.

They understand the simple rule ... Sell when prices are high and buy when they come down.

"If a little money does not go out, great money will not come in."
- Confucius.

Leisurely drip investing brings rich return. Buying a few shares, each time a well-researched companies price falters, will bring super returns to the wise investor ... Cream will always rise to the surface.

Each Precious Moment

In the cool damp haze of a morning mist,
Light filters powder diamond covered meadows,
This unfamiliar spring day stretches and yawns.

Inside vermilion dreams and crimson reality mingle in lucid complexions
Eyes slowly focus towards the open window of infinite opportunities
The world outside awakens to the milieu of songbirds serenade.

Tranquil connection effectuate sacred blessings
Gentle breezes, caress the cheek, a fresh horizon is born.
Legions of ideas await the golden enterprises of the day.

Each precious moment becomes a priceless treasured Gem.

The Billionaire Beggar

It was a fine morning and the sun was just starting out it daily journey seemingly moving from east to west. People were outside in the fine dawn air taking their morning walk. A few highly energetic folks were jogging along the sidewalk. All of them passed by a well dressed beggar who would greet them all with a beaming smile and a "Good Morning this fine day" Most would ignore him, but a few would reply back good morning to you. Just a handful would reach into their pockets and give the beggar a few dollars.

The beggar became a permanent fixture sitting on a sidewalk bench-wishing folks good morning, and the folks that gave him any money became less and less. However, one kind lady noticed nobody was giving him anything so she increased the money she gave him even though she could hardly afford to do so.

Then, one morning as the lady was putting her dollars into the hand of the beggar he gently held her wrist and placed a check into it. She looked at it and she smiled, for it read... "Pay the bearer $1,000,000. She remarked it was a nice gesture and only wished it were true. The beggar stood up, pulled out a cell phone and quickly made a call. Within one minute, a new chauffeur driven Rolls Royce came to a halt beside them. The chauffeur got out and said.... Are you ready to go home sir? He gave the woman a big hug and whispered in her ear...You have a good heart and a kind soul and the million dollars is your reward for giving when nobody else did. When we give from the heart and not because we want our name in lights, our rewards come back to us in many unexpected ways.

Autumn in Spring

Why are the leaves falling,
from those few trees in spring,
asks dis-gusted evergreens, to all their associates,
a pow-wow of all the normal trees was called,
the council of sophisticate brainy trees,
sentenced all the spring leaf-falling trees to death,
because they could not function like a normal tree,
thank goodness ... humans aren't as unfeeling as trees.

The Wizards Secret Power

In a small chocolate box cabin, on the edge of an obscure forest dwells a wizard with an incredible secret power. One day, he was meandering along a winding path deep in the forest when he came upon a broody, unhappy boy who was sitting on a log. Resting his elbows on his knees, he held his head in his hands and appeared to be very miserable indeed.
"Why the grim look?" ... asked, the wizard.
There was no reply...just a feeble grunt and weighty sigh!

"Come over here young man and look at this very old tree."
The boy stood up still looking glum and with his head hung low   .
meandered over to the wizard. "This tree has been around for many hundreds of years and never has it been sad for one moment. I have learnt its secret, therefore I am going to share with you the greatest gift any human can possess, but before I do, you must first complete a mission I will present to you.... "

"I know today is your twelfth birthday...You must keep a smile on your face for one year and never moan or groan. I will be following you around in my invisible form. When you feel the whiff of a breeze on your face, you will sense my presence. The very first time you stop smiling, moan or groan I will disappear forever and you will never know my secret power that will pass over to you next year. You will lose the greatest gift on earth and will be just like all the other mortals that live a wretched unhappy life."

The young boy eyes began to water and tears fell down his cheek like a waterfall cascading down a mountainside.
"That is good sign", remarked the wizard.
"Get rid of all your pent-up tension and unhappiness.
Remember this...You have but one life on earth and you cannot afford to spend one moment in misery.
From this moment on you will be conscious of the smile on your face and you will understand that if the smile fades for just one moment, you will lose contact with me and the secret power that I will bestow on you in a years time, will be lost, like a snowflake in a fire."

The boy's tears suddenly dried-up and a radiant smile beamed bright. Suddenly a strong wind blew and all the fallen leaves scattered all around the young boy. When the wind subsided, the wizard was gone.

38

The boy felt rejuvenated and although all the worries and problems he had still existed, his disposition was quite different. He launched into a merry jog and sang a happy song as he made his way out of the forest and back to his home to confront his problems and resolve outstanding issues.

Every morning, upon awakening he would go over to the mirror and make sure his smile was still in place. It seemed to get bigger and brighter every day...As the smile grew brighter, his demeanor, conduct and manner improved. Everyone remarked how different he was. Some mean spirited people tried to change his smile into a frown, but none could. It was engraved on his face like an exquisite incandescent photo.

At the end of the year, the wizard suddenly appeared from out of the blue and declared...
"Your disposition and nature has been extraordinarily noticeable.
Your luminous smile is a joy for all folks to behold.
I will now share with you the greatest secret power in the world that I possess."
The excited teenager held his breath in anticipation

"The truth of the matter is ... I do not have any secret power more potent than the one you possess.
The smile you have on your face right now is the greatest power in the world.
Once your face radiates with joy, you are empowered with the greatest gift any human can possess whilst they live on earth.
Now that you have experienced that power, I know there will be no going back to your old worried frown."

The young mans faced beamed even brighter and he threw his arms around the wizard and gave him a loving hug..."I thought that was going to be the secret. I am so glad that I will not be disappointed and given some golden magic charm or trinket."

As he hugged the wizard, a strong gust sprung up... lo and behold... he was left giving himself a big hug.

"I wonder if I have been having a dream," he thought... just then, a light breeze tickled his cheek and shivers ran down his spine like a mild electric current... This lit up his face more than ever and he said aloud ... Today I am thirteen years of age and the gift I want more than anything else is to find out how many people I can help smile today! All at once, he realized he had become a wizard on his thirteenth birthday.

The Thinker of the Thought

Reflections of the mind
in a life beyond earths green meadows,
My, how a seasons dramas pass by
like wind driven clouds,
And how congested the thinker of the thought.

Oceans shimmer like diamond starlight,
Mountain tops hide in silvery mystical haze,
Shadows stretch, tinted by crimson sunsets
varnishing the deep forests of pleasure,
Laughter and color frolic in twilight skies.

Beauty and joy dance in ever increasing circles
around the genius of fresh life,
Animals and plants live here
feeding each others existence,
Streams of exotic light infuse all.

But; how did it all slip by unnoticed?
Divine emptiness now fills the eternal voids,
A speck of mysterious nothingness reminisces,
Gazing,
Towards a place, of awe and wonderment.

Sailing the Seven Seas of Life

When we arrive into this world, we enter as a ship that navigates by the forces of nature and propelled by the power in the invisible auras of Spirit. It takes a few years for us to launch our ship with a self-propelled man made motor. During this process, we are taken to many shipyards for a refit to our intellect's knowingness. We are trained by man-made ideologies and our natural awareness starts to go down deep inside the "Davy Jones locker" within us. We are taught to accept a new identity that will become the captain of our ship. We have to pass many tests of approval by our Admiralty of mis-guided intellects. Once we believe we are qualified to be our own pilot and navigator, we set out to chart our voyage of a lifetime.

As we sail along on the sea of life's journey, we stop at many ports of call to pick up passengers and cargo. Some of these passengers become permanent guests in our lives. Some come for a short trip as they were sent to us to fill a need. Our thoughts advertised we were in need of advice and guidance so they came along for that part of our journey, for they knew the waters we were sailing. They steered us clear of dangers and helped us weather passing storms. Then they went on their way. Some died of a sickness or old age, but their souls stay with us for guidance, as long as we know where they are located in our inner sanctuary. They are the angels that we asked to help steer our course. We still have our trusted physical crew all around our ship, and we have to be aware that we need to treat them with love and respect or else we may encounter a mutiny.

We should always be on guard, for there are dangerous sharks and pirates in these waters. Many are after our cargo of money and treasures, whilst a few wish to take the joy out of our lives. The stock market is a vast ocean of scurvy forces that lie in wait to ambush us when we have lost our direction. There are many other unknown, hazardous ships, we will encounter on our travels and many fly the flag of friendship from a distance, but when we get up close, they hoist the skull and crossbones. Our lookouts fell asleep and we were attacked because impostors penetrated our vigilance. Enemies posing as friendly sailing vessels, in the seas turbulent cross currents of information. And so, we battle the storm and survive, but each battle leaves its scars on our vessel.

Once we journey beyond our half way mark, we suddenly get the feeling we might be heading in the wrong direction. We start to understand the real enemy is within our own ship, and the pilot we have so much faith in is an impostor. It is the same type of impostor that we have been battling in the other pirate ships, only this foe was planted in our thoughts for many years and has grown in stature and strength. So much so it thinks it can control the ship in heavy raging seas, even when it knows the ship is aging and does not have the power it once had. When it realizes it does not have any real power, it wants to abandon the ship as it begins to sink. It wants to forsake the vessel and allow it to crash on the rocks of worry and anxiety.

The captain of our ship is a wimp. A false-hearted scalawag, with no care for anything, except its own importance. It is a stowaway, which dresses up in a captain's uniform recognized by society's elite and panders to their whims. That is why we believed it to be so real, for we have all been flying the wrong flags, because our captains are nothing but sophisticated, adulterated, decoys. The real captain named Soul is still onboard but held captive in the deep recesses of our vessel.

Captain Ego needs to retire and become a quiet member of the crew.

The time has come to unlock the chains of imprisonment and allow our authentic, trusted captain to gain mastery of the controls of our ship. To escort us to safe waters, where we can float on a tide of supreme bliss. Each day we will set out to achieve new goals and visit places beyond distant horizons. We will still encounter many storms along our cruises but with a steadfast captain at the helm, we will never fear any assault on our peace and tranquility. We have a twenty-four hour watch in the crow's nest. Our finely tuned awareness is enjoying the true order of command. We have turned off the old worn out motor and we are sailing into the sunset with Spirit's forces supervising our sail.

Within our life span, everyone will sail the seven seas. We come into this world as a newborn baby and some of us leave within a day or two. We have still sailed the seven seas, only we did it in a pure vessel and in super fast time. Others may sail for over one hundred years. The time-scale is not that important. The quality and value of time spent joyfully is important.

The seas are the same for everyone. Only the time frame is a little longer for some. In cosmic terms, there is little difference in a second or a hundred years. The first taste is the banquet. The first sail is the experience of a lifetime. So we sail the seven seas of life, until the time comes to set our ship adrift. We then sail into the infinite calm waves, in the imponderable galax-seas of eternity. Until that day comes, let's sail our charter on the authentic sensations of love & joy. Only Spirit can award us with a true captain and navigator. Allow each moment to become a soul-filled adventure of unsurpassable bliss.

Glazed Eyes

An empty canvas permeated, with pure potential,
overflowing, with expectations,
colors, await their cue, to perform artistic grandeur,
brush strokes, asleep; dreaming visions,
 in multi-faceted dimensions,
aspirations of glazed eyes,
 will soon discover, their muse's intent.

Glazed eyes wonder... when will the picture take shape?
The canvas whispered... it was tinted, before you were born,
But, where will the picture come from? asked, the gazed eyes,
From me, the one who loves you dearly, replied the mystical muse,
Who can unite and compose with you? the glazed eyes enquired,
Each and every person, with white teeth...even if they are false teeth!

Music Maestro Please

Neil Armstrong walked on the moon and declared - One small step for man, one giant leap for humankind. The first human footprint imprinted on the moon and will forever be a monument to the ingenuity of the human race. That one small step by Mr. Armstrong is an exceptional feat of humanity's ingenuity. However, there is one small step backwards that very few human beings will ever experience in their life on earth and it is far more meaningful than walking on the Moon. What is it? Well, let me explain...

Some children become the center of attraction as soon as they walk into a room. While other children hide behind books or just sit as quietly as a mouse, so nobody will ask them to perform any childlike magic. As children grow into adulthood, it is not always the pushy kids, who make a success out of life. I guess success is the hardest commodity for anyone to define per se. It all depends on a person's standards, goals and inner feeling of prosperity. Certainly, money alone is no criteria for success. Neither is fame, for history has taught how the mighty have fallen.

When a human being matures into adulthood, they have a self-image which projects throughout their lives. The intellectual image that is set in the mind from childhood becomes the 'real person' and although it contains many role-plays, the identity image is fixed like a girder in cement. The human mind mistakenly interprets the world it sees by the reference points it has built-up over many years.

The ego/intellect becomes so real that any attempt to dislodge its hold on the mind is met with a fierce conscious defiance. A personal ego/intellect will never willingly give up its ground that has been cemented in place by all the reality that has been absorbed throughout its sight, hearing, touch, taste and feel in a three dimensional world. This is all it knows...This is all it believes to be correct, moral and principled or visa-versa. A small amount of the input is authentic, but a large percentage is bogus information.

The informed and educated adult intellect/ego feels it has a sound basis for projecting its own input into the human mish-mash of opinions, beliefs, notions, perceptions, concepts, thoughts and knowledge. Often this is backed-up by scholastic degrees and awards. How sound are all these beliefs and convictions?

Well, the results of a person's life will speak for itself. It is not the opinion of others who will determine whether a life on earth was worthwhile and authentic. Rather, it is only the person themselves that can give an honest appraisal as to the richness, fruitfulness, prosperity, comfort, joy and tranquility of their life.

The question to ask oneself is… Have I truly been the maestro of the orchestrations in my life or have I let other people conduct all my compositions without any of my own legitimate personal input. Indeed, what does it mean being the maestro of one's own life?

To find the answer to that question a person needs to be able to take one small step backwards in time and space, so that they view their own life as an observer, rather than the participant. To be able to get a constructive view of ones own life the person needs to determine accuracy's as an alternative to misrepresentations and that is impossible if we believe we already know the answer by the sole view of our own intellect/ego.

Do you feel a little mystified? Of course, you do and it is normal reaction when something does not fit into your perspectives ... because, who is it in your mind that is interpreting this essay you are reading? Why lo and behold, it is your very own intellect/ego and it may strongly disapprove of what it is reading. After all, how can it possible admit to being a false participant in your life when everything seems so steadfast and credible from its point of view. This is where the alchemist in you may begin to stir from the slumber.

So, are you the innocent victim of a case of mistaken identity built by your ego/intellect or do you have the potential to become the majestic maestro of your life concert?

Being the conductor of a social orchestra means encompassing the super-vision of every player you meet and greet. With baton in hand, the maestro will generate music that warms the heart and soothes the soul. Of course, conducting great music is to no avail if there is no audience in the theater to soak up the symphonic ambiance.

There is…
A time for sitting in the audience,
A time for playing in the orchestra,
A time for composing music,
A time for becoming the maestro,

Sitting in the arena of life fashions every human being as the audience and no matter how great their position in society, most of the time, they are listening to other people perform their roles. At some point most people will be given a chance to play their instrument, i.e., Get up out of their seat and 'make their presence felt' through their career, family or other society roles. For instance, even the humblest of shop assistants are given the chance to perform for many customers each and every day. That is their audience and they can charm them into enjoying their purchase or bore them into leaving empty handed.

As life progresses and they become more experienced, there will be an opportunity for them to take the baton and become the maestro. It is their turn to take charge and make their purpose in life ring with the harmonious bells of true prosperity...The more they please their audience the better the acclamations and kudos. Monetary wealth accumulates with little or no effort, because that was not the sole purpose of the works... Enjoyment of the job-in-hand and helping other people, to enjoy the experience, was there primary motivation.

By taking the one small step backwards, you will make a gigantic leap towards the most incredible life on earth you could ever imagine. A life that embraces all things bright and beautiful no matter how much darkness and ugliness they contain.
•• Seeing the good in the people that normally irritate and vex
•• Extracting positive energy when doing tasks and chores that would normally transfer negative fatigue
•• Enjoying the disappointments and expectations that did not materialize as anticipated
•• Loving exploring the unknown challenges that seem so far out of reach at this moment in time
•• Holding out the mental arms of compassion and grace so that the burdens of depression and worry can be lifted from other peoples lives

The baton of time is swinging over your head. It is held in place for you by the master maestro of the universe. Before you can accept the baton you need to take that one small step backwards and become directly in-tune with universal intelligence. By serving your authentic purpose of life, you become the instrument of the genius of the soul. Now, the intellect/ego has a true foundation to soak up all the learning and education is has absorbed over the years and put it to good use for the betterment of humanity.

The transformation may not be that apparent to most people, but you will know the difference you feel and the bliss you experience every moment of every day. You may not obtain fame and fortune, but you recognize you hold the wise treasures of the universe in the center of your heart. You possess the wisdom gems of the cosmos in the center of your gut...And you know beyond doubt, you carry the infinite-sacred-divine in the center of your mind...

Music maestro please!

Professional Optimist

Professional transparent optimists,
view life, in tinctures of plumb mirth,
Presented, in dribbling pink merriment,
moments, gleaming in pastel goo-goos,
Polished, in scarlet orgasmi-comical splendor
Life is...
Dusky business, for the worrisome staid,
verses....
Illuminating hobbies, for the crystalline simple,
Heavy work, for the exasperated serious,
verses....
Light play-time, for the translucent wholesome,
What's your favorite cup-of-flavor?

Part Two - Overture To Health Alchemy

Balancing the Scales of Thought

When I was a little boy, one of my treats was to go to the local candy store and get my penny bag of candy. I went into the store and looked around at all the fabulous glass jars of candy on the shelves and the aroma of all the flavors sent me on a trip of delights.

I now had to choose which jar of candy I would like – a tough decision for a six year old with only one penny to spend (well, it was over fifty years ago). Once I pointed to the jar that was making my mouth water, the old man would take the jar off the shelf, unscrew the lid and carefully weigh out a few ounces of candy on the little scales. A four-ounce weight went on one side and the candy sprinkled on the other. I thought him to be a mean old man, for not one fraction of an ounce was given away. The scales had to balance exactly on the mark.

The amount of candy I bought for one penny was just the correct amount to last me through the week. I would eat a few pieces each day and at the end of the week I would eat my last piece and it was time for my allowance of one penny again.

There were a few occasions when I received a little extra money from an uncle or aunt. I would buy a huge bag of candy and stuff them down all at once. Rolling round the room with stomachache and a few bouts of being sick soon cured that. I realized very early that you can have too much of a good thing.

If the old man in the candy store would have tipped the scales and given me more candy I guess, I may have been sick more often. I realize now he was being kind to me by balancing the scales spot on and not giving me more than my allotted share. It is indeed a shame that greed has become so fashionable these days.

Balance in all things is the correct way to live. So how do we balance our scales to get the correct perspective of life?

Allowing time-out to sit in silence, so that our mind can relax from all the pressures that modern living brings, will help us find inner peace. Every human being can locate a source of information and wisdom that has shaped the authentic side of humanity over millions of years. If our thoughts and actions do not bring true joy, without any materialistic attachments, then they may not contain too much genuine meaning.

To obtain the sweetness life has to offer we cannot afford to unbalance our scales (mind) or we will become frustrated and angry. We must weigh up each situation that comes into our lives and balance our thinking, so that we understand what feels good and what does not.

Our candy shop is the world we live in. We are born into a magical globe called earth, full of beauty and bliss. We are intoxicated with all the aromas and visions of all the candies of nature. We only need our fair measure of wealth, brought to us by the fruits of our labor. Too much will make us sick. If we think we have too little, we will think life is mean and build jealousy and hatreds.

Balancing the scales of thought to embrace the joys of a human experience is taught through the guidance of inner wisdom that encompasses the human spirit.
It makes winners from the 'also rans'...Even if they did not finish in first place. It allows all humans to live as equals with no divisions from personal view-points, color, creed, religion or any (non) belief systems

As we learn to embrace the gift of being alive on earth's wondrous playground, our love and joy will spread out to reach everyone we meet and greet. The non-tangible delights and succulent invisible treasures of a human life will last us until the day we leave for the next journey somewhere beyond the beyond.

We only have a small allowance of time on earth....... We should spend it wisely.

A True Heart

Ah! The whispers within mist-tickle trees,
Enchanted forests of neurons cultivated in delicate-seas,
Radiance of light beams through the haze,
Hidden mysteries, as our free-path snakes a myriad of ways.

No; this is no pastoral scene,
It all takes place in a daytime dream,
It is called life, a domicile within our mind,
A home where, truth, is so hard to find.

Only when we discover, expressions, beyond be-lie-f.
And grasp time, from the clutches, of a habituated thief,
Only then, will we realize that; there is no need to endure,
A devil of a mind ... that rejects heartfelt universal law.

The law that wills ... there is just love & joy,
A work of art, so simply graceful, that one's spirit can employ,
To enhance a soul that nourishes, a medley of breeds,
With a true heart, that sows a fellowship, of natures-natural-seeds.

A Fish With Big Ideas

Simon was a little fish with big ideas. He lived in the deep waters of a large ocean that was not charted on any map. The reason being, human beings had yet to become an animal that lived on earth. In fact, there were no animals or birds on earth, for most of the surface were covered with salt water.

When Simon was just a little toddler, he loved to swim and frolic with all the other deep-water fish. However, as he began to mature into a teenage fish he started to wonder where all the light beams that shone down on him through all the darkness came from.

Some days it was very dismal indeed, whilst other days the waters seem to illuminate with a fascinating glow. He soon realized the closer he swam to the surface, the brighter it would become. However, all the other older fish told him he must not go too near the surface; otherwise, he would perish from too much light. You see, they were also told by their parents that too much light will destroy them, so they always feared the light and stayed deep in the water where very little light shone down from above.

Simon would have none of their superstitious fears, for when he grew bigger and stronger; he left his family and began to live much closer to the surface. One day he met another fish named Suzy and found love, joy and synchronicity with each other at first sight. They became fish soul mates and swam everywhere together.

One day Simon and Suzy both thought it would be a good idea to see if they could jump out of the water, from beneath the surface, to get a quick glimpse of what it was like to experiencing pure daylight. They were very adventurous. Simon and Suzy thought similar thoughts and wanted to explore everything they could.

So they took a big deep fish breath and holding fins they leapt out of the water together and seemed to fly in the air for a few moments before plunging back below the surface. Wow! That was the most exhilarating experience they ever savored in their short lives. Repeatedly they sprung from the depths and into the glorious sunlight. Day-by-day they were able to stay out of the water a little longer and could fly further above the surface.

One evening when they were enjoying their evening meal of plankton, they both wished they could sprout wings and fly. They knew if their secret wish was revealed to any other fish, they would be ridiculed and become a laughing stock. Every moment they focused their thoughts together as one being and imagined flying through the air and never returning to the water.

A few years went by ... Simon and Suzy had become fully-grown fish. They continued to enjoy their fun and games of flying above the surface of the water for a few seconds and then returning. One day something different happened. Like a miracle, when they started to fly, lo and behold, they flew higher and higher. They began to glide through the air on wind currents. All of a sudden, they discovered their dreams and wishes had come true. Simon and Suzy had sprouted wings and they could fly through the air with the greatest of ease.

After a while, they spotted land ... An island with an abundance of trees and plants with delectable berries. A miracle had indeed occurred ... Because they persisted in their belief that one day they could fly; amazingly, they had transformed themselves into birds.

Simon and Suzy were the first birds on earth. They had found a paradise island that supplied all their food and shelter. As time progressed, the couple produced a large family. Perhaps the birds you see in the sky today were fashioned because, two little fish with big ideas, had a great thought. They understood that all creative thoughts come from an infinite source of intelligence that can create and evolved all manner of creatures large and small.

Just ponder for a few moments what a fantastic miracle it is, that a spinning rock in space, metamorphosed itself into a superabundant paradise called earth. Look around the country at the beauty of the mountains, lakes, flowers and trees. Look in the shopping mall stores at all the ingenuity of humanity... Take a look at all the super products and produces you can purchase... Everything you see came from nothingness. Live alchemy ideas, which amazingly manifest from… universal intelligence. Some of it is artificial products, most of it nature made, but all of it came from the same source of intelligent ideas.

Also, just ponder for a few moments... If your father did not have a wink in his eye and an amorous thought in his mind, his sperm may not have entered your mother's egg. You may never have existed if a thought in your parents mind did not turn into an act of lovemaking. The minuscule one cell they reproduced had access to all the intelligence of the universe. Moreover, that one little cell that reproduced itself into billions of cells is now you in all your grown-up glory, which still has access to infinite universal intelligence. The only thing that can block your connection is your intellect/ego.

The potency of thought is very powerful, and if it can turn a fish into a bird. Just think what a wonderful, spectacular utopia, every human being can turn their lives into. All it takes is a vivid imagination and a continuing-conscious-connection to the creator/evolver of all things bright and beautiful.

"Until one is committed, there is hesitancy, the chance to draw back, always ineffectiveness. Concerning all acts of initiative and creation, there is one elementary truth the ignorance of which kills countless ideas and splendid plans: that the moment one definitely commits oneself, then providence moves too. All sorts of things occur to help one that would never otherwise have occurred. A whole stream of events issues from the decision, raising in one's favor all manner of unforeseen incidents, meetings and material assistance, which no man could have dreamed would have come his way. Whatever you can do or dream you can, begin it. Boldness has genius, power and magic in it. Begin it now." _ Attributed to Goethe?

Nature's Delicacies

In the land of garlic mountains
and olive oil lakes,
wholesome little souls
dwell in smooth,
bitter-sweet chocolate cabins,

On romantic gingerbread paths
matchbox donkeys meander into
music box towns,

Cheerful candy floss clouds float over
mellow orchid harbors,
powdered with elegant cinnamon sailing boats,

Nature's heavenly delicacies
savors so sublime
ambrosial delights divine

A Long Life

For hundreds of years Jewish people have blessed others who have
recently buried a loved one with the saying ... 'I wish you a long Life.'
Why is it that most human beings do not get the chance to blow out the
candles on their hundredth birthday cake? Statistics state not too many
people live passed eighty. Many trees and plants have a far more
prolonged life than humans. Indeed there are a multitude of animals, fish
and birds that have a longer life-span than humans. For example;
•• Giant Tortoise (average life-span of about 200 years)
•• Oregon Sturgeon (average life-span of about 150 years)
•• Eastern Box Turtle (average life-span of about 123 years)
•• Egyptian Vulture (average life-span of about 118 years)

If animals, birds and fish can outlive humans without getting sick and
going to a doctor for pills, we must have got our intelligence all mixed up
in a conceited maze of refined intellectual thinking. Could it be we really
do not need to die a premature death from disease? Do we have no option
than to declare there is no other choice than intermittent illness throughout
our lifetime, leading to an early grave? A few people do live to a ripe old
age because they inherited strong genes and DNA. But, leaving that aside,
how does the average person live in good health, to a fully developed old
age, as nature intended?

I guess most folks believe that our "advancements' in the world of science
and medicine have increased our life expectancy. This is true to some
extent, but it is only true in the context of keeping us alive in ill-health,
despite our continuous bad habits and erroneous lifestyles. We can
alleviate the effects of an illness, but the cause lingers on, brings an
uncomfortable life and will eventually lead to a premature, distressing
passing. So what can be done to remedy the situation of being a pawn in a
commercial chess game of beggar thy neighbor, performed in a worldwide playhouse?

Firstly, if we stop polluting the earth with poisonous gasses, pesticides and
a multitude of other pollutants we would need fewer drugs to sustain our
lives. Therefore, it seems sensible to stop corporations from manufacturing
pollutants because of their need to feed the greed of a few humans who
hold stocks in their companies. In addition, self-pollution is an outstanding
problem and banning smoking in all public places is a must-do and long
overdue action.

The next move in the appropriate direction to a longer healthier life would be to educate folks on the correct foods to eat and liquids to drink. Pure water should be the principal drink and alcohol consumption should be restricted to three glasses of wine a week at the most.

All our dietary needs can be supplied with simple yet delicious whole foods, herbs and spices, which are heart healthy and loved by every cell in our bodies. Our minds are constantly brainwashed by the advertising media educating our taste buds to enjoy refined foods contain high levels of sugar, salt, hydrogenated fats and other harmful "tasty stuff." These foods are usually all dressed up with colorants and artificial flavors. What a concoction of poison we have produced for ourselves. In addition, we pay good money to eat foods that bring about illness, which inconveniently installs us in a box six foot under the ground; before our shelf life was due to expire.

Regular exercise can help elevate the onset of many dis-eases… Here again, simplicity is the key. Walking and swimming are two of the easiest and most enjoyable forms of exercise available to most folks. A few weight-bearing exercises are also useful to keep muscle tone and bone strengthening.

However, the most important ingredient in living a long and healthy life is the way we think. What we need to ask ourselves is "Who is it that resides inside my head that makes all the decisions for me." If our minds have become too refined, just like the refined junk foods, which we eat ... that has the wholesome goodness removed ... we will be left with junk-intellectual- thoughts.... Sophisticatedly refined, but good -for-nothing... A strong spiritual soul will never allow that to happen.

Once we start to recognize the true soulful genius that we authentically are ... that lives outside our ego's perceptions and opinions ... we will start to change our way of thinking and will live to the maximum of our allotted life-span. It could well be we live to 120 years of age in good health, if we do not allow negative, erroneous thoughts to upset the balance that nature has so magnificently provided for us all.

If we could only come to realize that we are a cog in the wheel of nature and if we desire that wheel to keep on turning effortlessly, we must become one with all that exists on earth.

56

The sands of time in humanities hourglass is quickly running out and unless we make the correct lifestyle changes, there will not be any life left here on earth for future generations to enjoy. So let's take a leaf out of the book of the Giant Tortoise and slow down the runaway intellectual human brain, so that we enjoy our swim in the ... Quantum Universe of Infinite Joy here on earths de-light-ful playground.

The Viewer of the View

I am a majority of nothing
I count for minus one
I am a witness to everything
an observer of three dimensional illusions
that cast shadowed trails to follow
into fabricated concoctions
embellished with assumptions and perceptions
via theories, thesis and speculative postulation
all posing as the truth
all demanding attention in war like garb
Without emotion, I am the viewer of the view
I exist beyond the thinker of the thought
and can testify to...the squander of time.

Scuffed Shoes

How many mothers make sure their children wear the correct size shoes and modern style? They go to great lengths in instructing them not to scruff their new shoes or else there will be all hell to pay. Of course, the first day on, they go to school and come home with their shoes all scuffed up.

This leads to many shouting bouts, much anxiety and lots of aggravation for the devoted mum.....Low and behold, before-you-know-it, the little scamps have grown out of their shoes and they have to be discarded and thrown in the garbage (the shoes, not the kids).

In life, we will eventually be discarded everything we hold onto and safeguard. Even our bodies, no matter how well we look after them, will turn into dust and even the dust will fade into nothingness. So why get all hot and bothered about anything that has a temporal nature ...Yes, I can hear you say...its all-right for him to say that, but he does not have my worries.

I doubt if there is one person on earth who does not have to face daily challenges to their sanity and wellbeing. It is not the devastations and worries we need to deal with...it is how we deal with our own perspectives and viewpoints that makes all the difference. And that can never be found in the main stream intellectual reasoning of any human being...for to reason away one crisis, and treat it with medication or surgery, will only bring about another unexpected desperate episode that stumps the wicket keeper.

The only way to keep playing the game and enjoying the results is to go out into the world and get your shoes all scuffed up. In other words, enjoy your life and when the wrinkles start to appear on your face, make sure they are laughter lines and don't let cosmetic surgery cover up your happiness. Keep your mind and body healthy by recognizing the person you are, before your personality and ego fashioned itself...Then act out your role-plays on earth with the guidance of the universal wizard that exists behind the easily provoked, personality masquerade.

Enjoy your kids growing-up...Enjoy their wedding day... Enjoy your retirement and before you know it, you will be six feet under enjoying turning to dust....I guess even then, some anxious souls will be still be worrying and fussing....trying to clean-up the dust in their coffin?

Somebody's Divine Lifetime
Tranquil inspirations of creation
award a serene dawn,
in order that mortal reservations can
rent, unstoppable time and earth bounded space

Each splendorous year is akin
to one divine sentence,
of the blessed first page,
in the sacred transient book of existence

One astonishing life equals one miraculous page,
as each incredible leaf turns,
one fantastic light dims,
another spectacular light rekindles in fresh garb,

Life; 'tis but a brief spark of excellence,
an exquisite luminosity,
filled with exciting adventures,
mysterious myths,
 'n delicious creativity

Surrounded by velvet darkness,
enveloped in incredible curiosity,
not a flicker must blow in provocative annoyance,
or preposterous bedevilment of insane dogma,

Grace's phenomenal coloring,
joy's pleasurable gloss,
love's heavenly fragrance,
all, fuel the radiance of someone's gratifying existence

One page that signifies somebody's divine lifetime,
beautifully embossed and engraved in.........
Awesome, wondrous bliss,
This is your book of life.

Applause, Applause

I'd like to wager you're not aware that you're performing to a captive audience every minute of every day, ever since you were born. Yep, your audience hangs on your every word...hovers over every thought. Nothing you do escapes their attention. There are no auditions and every action is absorbed ...What's that you say...you do not believe me? Well, I can assure you it's true. In fact, your audience is far larger than the human population of the world. They will applaud and cheer your deliberations, or boo and hiss your thoughts and there is not a thing you can do about their reactions.

Wait a minute; come to think about it, there is something you can do. First, I suppose I'd better let you know who your audience is...It is every cell in your body and mind. You have over several trillion of the little mites and over a hundred trillion bacteria cells. They will let you know in-no-uncertain-terms how you are performing your roles on earth. All will be reflected in your health.

For every negative thought you have, you will lose some of your precious, beloved supporters and give strength to the bad guys, who have only come along to help you fall frail and die of a disease. Their only mission in life it to take you to the grave as early as possible.

For every erroneous thought you feed them, they will react in a destructive manner and will attack all your good guys. It seems on the surface, according to the experts, you are helpless to do anything about them. That is because many medical, educated people will tell you it is perfectly normal for cells to be destroyed by disease and in most cases, they do not know where the illness originated. They will inform you that ... human emotions are real and since they are real, only medication or mediation (science or religion) will help cool them down.

What they will not inform you, because most of them do not know, it is the authentic you, that is filled with universal intelligence, that can help yourself overcome your ego's requirements for power and destruction... However, before that alchemical intelligence can perform its magic, the ego needs to understand its purpose... and unfortunately it is beyond its intellectual grasp. Therefore, most people's intellectual egos govern how much ammunition the detrimental cells absorb...

"Whosoever wishes to know about the world, must learn about it in its particular details.

60

Knowledge is not intelligence.
In searching for the truth, be ready for the unexpected.
Change alone is unchanging.
The same road goes both up and down.
The beginning of a circle is also its end.
Not I, but the world says it: all is one.
And yet everything comes in season." - Heraklietos of Ephesos.

Human negative emotions, governed by the intellect, seem so real, but they are not real, they are all figments of the ego's hold on the mind. However, as-long-as people believe educated intellectual experts that lack universal intelligence and abound in all walks of life.... Then the negative emotions will be viewed as real sentiments that need pandering and loving care....Nothing can be further from the truth and since people live the lies of the ego, and have done for thousands of years, there is no real hope or any authentic help for them.

Clinging on to figments erected by fallacious, educated thinkers only produces a human race that is overflowing with deceits, wars and self-inflicted disease.

Human negative emotions have been programmed in human DNA and genes over many millennia by past negative thinkers. In addition, numerous diseases are induced by a miscellany of ingredient, including environmental and genetic affects. However, it does not mean disease cannot be eradicated to a large extent, by a strong immune system that is regulated by an unfamiliar way of thinking that is authentic and as intelligent as time itself.

Most medical doctors (whose treatment is an essential necessity when we get sick) will prescribe drugs and medicine to help rid the body of disease. They ignore the fact the infected cells emanate from your brains erroneous thoughts...So, without doubt, you are the cause of your own illness. Not knowingly, or else you would not make yourself sick, or would you?

Do people who smoke cigarettes know they will probably die of lung cancer?

Do people who drink alcohol know they may die of an illness caused by the alcohol?
Do obese people know that overeating is shortening their lives?

What! They do know ... then why do they do it?
Why not arrest a bad habit if it detrimental for a persons health?

If only it was that simple to stop, but unfortunately it is not. Bad habits are hard to break simply because they are transported on incorrect thoughts ... They are the hardest of all to cure because they depend on a personal identity to support their addiction. Emotional stress, and negative thoughts, have become addictive and have spread like the plague throughout all humanity.

The emotions implanted in human minds are the number one source of deaths since humans evolved as sophisticated animals that can reason their existence. Over time, volumes of mistaken progressive logic and reason has radiated from science and religion ... The more conclusive and indisputable the effects became to each group, the more the drawbridge was pulled up on simple truths.

The modern day realities of the human race establish themselves and formulate at universities and places of learning. The purpose and application of "a sound education" for good intent has mostly evaporated into the red- hot domain of materialistic greed and ego building by degrees. You only have to read the daily papers to see how the leaders in politics, media, corporations, science and religions are using their inept, improper education to protect their ivory towers and inflict their fractious ideas and views on a downward spiraling world society.

Degrees and diplomas may signify and endorse a person's ability to read and write, but it also masks how things in the physical world do not add-up to produce a sound society. Education that lacks the wisdom in how to apply the knowledge within the universal laws of good intent can and does produce a world filled with attitudes of greed and beggar-thy-neighbor. A society that lacks grace and compassion is a society doomed for extinction.

The media and places of education are the greatest culprits in encouraging false ideas, concepts, opinions and beliefs, embedded in peoples ego's and there is little anyone can do to stop their unsound cavorting. The academic ivory tower brigade holds center stage. The intellectual people with power do not accept they could be close-minded and ignorant of universal intelligence.
However, there is something you can do to stop subscribing to the logic and reasoning of unwise educated people, who consider the three dimensional world their only reality. Intellect and Intelligence may be close stable mates; however, one is a Hacker, the other a Thoroughbred.

When people live with convictions that they believe hold all the truth, then for sure something will come along and prove their beliefs false. It may take thousands of years, or it may only take a few moments, but all certainties in a three dimensional world are held together by threads of veracity and filled in with illusionary fantasies and inventive imaginations.

Many years ago, doctors stuck leeches on their rich patients and used magic potions such as ground emeralds to heal? With the help of the educated quackery, the rich, sick people died faster than the sick poor people, who had no 'expert' help. At least today, you recognize the educated experts of old were quacks in white coats.

In today's world, medical practitioners keep people alive longer so that the drug companies can get richer and folk's quality of life becomes poorer..... The patients grow sicker by the side effects of the drugs which over time, require different drugs to treat the effects of the original drugs.....Good game for the doctors and drug companies, but hard cheese to the patient.... The funny thing is, most directors of the drug companies and doctors will succumb to the same types of disease as their patients. If they cannot help themselves, what chance does the public stand?

Let's get back to your inner audience...Your benevolent; chivalrous cells only want what is good for your welfare... They will produce spectacular encouragement within your immune system, just so long as you feed them the correct formula that they were naturally born to embrace. So, what is it that you can do, to assure good health throughout your lives and never need to visit the people in white coats, with sharp knives and laughing gas?

There is one golden rule to understand ... You are not your ego, personality, character, name, or any label that you hang your hat on... Nothing on this planet earth, in the physical, is part of your true self. If you cannot grasp this one golden rule, then nothing on earth will ever help you solve or cure, whatever troubles you have now, or in the future. Every negative habit depends on your identity within the mind's sentiments and emotions. Your personality cultivates the destruction of the cells in your body due to the harmful chemicals released by the emotions. Therefore, it cannot-be-stated strongly enough ... detrimental thoughts manufacture ... injurious chemicals.

Your eating habits are programmed into your taste buds, fed by your memories of what you believe you relish. Your exercise or laziness is a measure of your minds willingness to keep fit. Your worry, anxiety, hatreds and anger will all be triggered by the emotional storehouse in which your memory banks have invested their time observing and programming...Do you really want to live your life as a programmed puppet, at the mercy of every stranger who can pull your strings?

Deny your emotions their false reality and you will stop them from producing the harmful chemicals that can kill your adoring, good cell audience. Every thought you experience will spark neurons that will send messengers, to each selective cell member in your body. The chemical messengers will affect your health, for better or worse, until death you do depart. So, how's about you start to put on a new show filled with merriment and laughter.

Start to laugh at your own behavior and stubbornness. Ridicule yourself, mock yourself, mimic yourself. Make yourself a laughing stock, to yourself... Enjoy tearing your identity into little shreds of fiction they are and then bury the evidence in the deepest burial ground in your mind...never repossessed in the same form.... You begin to renew your self-image filled with feelings of love and joy and even though it is still a sham world you live in, you see its falseness and can enjoy its antics without any hindrance of being defensive....

You see yourself as a temporal being that is put on earth to enjoy life and nothing is going to take away your joy-filled self ... for that is your eternal true identity and thus indestructible. You can help other people by projecting your joy and living by the laws of good intent. You wish everyone well, and even those who want to demean you ... send them all your best.

Then, when anyone else comes along and derides you and tells you how dumb and silly you are, you can laugh with them and say...You know you are quite right and your inner audience will give you a rousing encore for the best performance of your life so far.
 You will find your acting gets better and better along with your well being. Your health, fame and wellness fortune will spread and enjoyed by every nurturing cell in your body and mind. The stimulation of your joyful energy becomes an intoxicating elixir of wisdom, filling all the gaps left behind by your old scallywag emotions of illusionary negativity....

Meet you at the interval for a cool glass of freshly squeezed orange juice and you can let me know how your audience is appreciating your new authentic inner-thespian.

64

Wisdom of Le Mer

Men in deck-chairs, sat on the beach,
each a world leader, in politics and religion,
one exclaimed................
The roar of the ocean, blocked out his intercourse,
not to be rude ... all approvingly nodded their heads in agreement,
each in turn, expressed their extreme, dogmatic viewpoints,
only to be drowned-out, by the thunder of the waves,
After a two hour debate,
unified, all jubilantly shook hands,
harmoniously hugged each other,
and agreed......
it was the most successful meeting ever held.

The Maintenance Wizard

If you own a modern computer, you will know there is a maintenance wizard in your windows software. With a click of the mouse, you can sit back whilst the wizard automatically checks out your computer for any faults. If it finds anything amiss, it will correct it within a few seconds. The wizard will also remove any files that are not necessary in its memory banks.

Wow! What a wizard... It would be great, if we had a wizard in our minds, which could remove sickness and rid all erroneous memories...A wholesome lifetime of never falling into ill health. Well, we do have such a wizard enmeshed in every human being. .....Just a minute, I can sense you do not believe what I am saying. Well, what I am saying does fly-in-the-face of modern conventional medical science. Non-the-less, if you live in true joy, you will never get sick.

What is he talking about I hear you say... I'm deep in debt... My son was sent home from school for being a disruptive influence... My beloved aunt is dying of cancer ... The boss is telling me business is slow and he may have to lay people off if things don't pick up... The roof is leaking and the dogs got diarrhea...There is also a hundred and one other problems piling up on the back cooker.

Quite so, everyone is faced with problematic challenges every day of their lives. That is all part of the human experience of living in a modern day world. The main problem is, the world we live in is no longer natural. It has become perplexingly plastic and sophisticatedly complex and if we accept it as our reality, we will have no chance of living a healthy dis-ease free life. Simplicity is the answer to many problems, but when given a choice of an easy way or a hard way to solve a problem, most "normal" people will take the hard egoistical route. Why? ... Because they live with an egotistical, intellectual master/monster, and it is his/her way or no-way.

But, what about God... Isn't 'he' supposed to help us live disease free? If he is watching over us, why is 'he' not listening to our prayers?
• Why is he slinging a deaf ear?
• Why is "he' allowing such suffering to all the kind innocent folks who are asking him for help?

As with everything else in our lives, the answer is simple but unacceptable to the conditioned minds of "normal" unnatural people. The Male God does not exist, that is why "he" cannot perform miracles and has not been seen nor heard from since the days of superstitions, fables, yarns, folklore and myths. Unfortunately, 'he' has been planted into the conditioned minds of robotic humans, who never ask profound questions that need truthful answers. Blind be-lie-fs will lead the followers into blind wars and blind self-inflicted-disease-destruction.

However, there is an infinite power that creates, organizes, nurtures, cultivates, nourishes and evolves all life forms animate and non-animate. We can call that intelligent energy God, but it does not require prayer because it has already given us everything we will ever want to live on earth in health, wealth, happiness, peace, serenity and harmony.

When human beings began to create their own individual power base to protect themselves from other tribes, all of humanities modern day woes began. The old saying "united we stand, divided we fall." are amongst the truest words ever spoken. Moreover, we will never be united as long as we are segregated by diverse doctrines of funny, bazaar, freakish man-made Gods. If people aren't killed in wars they will most certainly kill themselves by an inauthentic lifestyle. If they die of dis-ease, then in most cases it is a self-inflicted illness, brought on by erroneous, negative thoughts.

Wow! What's happened to the maintenance wizard? Have no fear; the wizard will not ever go away. It is part of whom and what we are, and it can repair all ills if caught in time and will delete all invaded programs if you allow it to perform its divine magic. All religions contain truths but they become distorted and erroneous once a human image of God materializes...God is not in human form and a human being has no more rights to an existence on earth than a worm or ant. All life come into being from nature's intelligence and all are equal in true essences of intelligent cosmic energy.

Our maintenance wizard is labeled 'soul' and it is the most misunderstood word on the human tongue. The soul possesses no negative emotions. It embodies feelings of love & joy in realms of intelligent non-visible indestructible energy. When we are aware of this life creating force, we live an authentic life on earth. We live as an ego, guided by the soul wizard and that makes us true human beings.

What about the guy with all the problems to solve who says he can't live in joy? Firstly, he needs remove his debt mountain of woes. Once the wizard gets to work, the debt will vanish...because s/he will understand it is not an option. If s/he can't afford non-essentials, then s/he does not buy them and s/he lives more simply, until the debt is paid off. Then, when s/he has saved up enough reserves, s/he can spend some money on a few luxury items and just as long as s/he never, ever goes back into the red, s/he will enjoy the wealth nature gives everyone freely.

As for the problem with the son that was sent home from school...He needs to detach from the conditioning the parents have most likely have taught him. He must now learn he is going to school to enjoy his learning and if the teachers do not know how to teach, he can become their mentor by excelling in all his subjects despite their lack of wisdom. The soul inner alchemy wizard... who has no human form... who cannot be overcome by pride and egoistical human non-sense, empowers him. Now, instead of being a disruptive influence, he becomes school leader, even if the other pupils and teachers cannot recognize it. Self-empowerment is not beholden to the opinion of others. At-the-same-time he is never rude or disrespectful. The real God within is in action and cannot be overcome by mortal stupidity. No buildings or holy books are required to replace the maintenance wizard. Everything authentic is pre-programmed in the subconscious mind and will click into action after the mind has rested in silence for a short period. The boy becomes a man of sincere heartfelt character and honest reputation.

What about the beloved aunt who is dying of cancer...Visit her in a state of happiness and joy. Understand there is no such thing as death in the real sense of the word. The wizard within is the true identity of every human. It is a speck of energetic, intelligent nothingness, which contains everything. This is our own true selves and it is the maintenance wizard, which can fix our mental computer, so that we can run on full power and vitality in perfect health. If the aunt has not gone down the path of illness too far, then there is a good chance she can recover from her illness, once she accepts her true identity. However, from my experience, when a person has journeyed down the wrong path for along period it is very difficult for them to re-arrange their thinking and mind conditioning, once illness has taken a firm hold and the mind has been weakened. It is far easier to prevent illness than to fix it when it strikes. The maintenance wizard will not let its computer down if it is permitted to carry out its

mission, with freedom and support from the mind and body that carries it.

We still have the boss to deal with whom threatening the layoffs. With the power of the wizard within, you will be the last person the boss will fire, because you have become an intricate, indispensable part of the business and will bring it back to profitability. In no-time-at-all you will become the CEO and sack the boss who could not run things efficient or effectively.

As for the roof that is leaking... ring up a roofing contractor and let him use his roofing wizardry to fix your roof. Before you contact him, go around the neighborhood and find houses with new roofs. Knock on doors and find the best contractor who does the best job at the most reasonable price. You can be sure his wizard is in good working order.

We still have the dog's diarrhea to clear up. Well...there are many messes that happen in our lives and sometimes we just have to roll up our sleeves and clear up the muck left by others. Just be thankful we're not elephant keepers.

Nature's Friend

Not that you would call
him a hermit or recluse,
but he had no time
for small talk or gossip,
certainly, he could not be
regarded as a social animal,
he loved nothing better
than to ramble through
the countryside in early spring,
to greet and meet
millions of new buddies.

Animal Awareness

Scientists are sending rockets into deep space so that six months later they can dispatch a torpedo into a comet, to cause an explosion they can study. Perhaps after the recent tidal wave disaster they should probe human nature a little more closely and turn their attention to humanity's inner space or human beings' lack of awareness to nature's dangers....

The Tsunami that hit Asia came as a complete surprise to humans. All the animals in the area, however, ran to higher ground many hours before the tidal waves struck. Their acute awareness of danger alerted them and they never questioned its authenticity. They did not need a second opinion from some other source of information.

When the four hurricanes hit Florida last season wild animals, birds and butterflies took shelter well before the storms struck. Even sharks swam out into deeper waters to avoid being swept ashore by a possible tidal wave. Being particularly aware of all dangers that could unfold, they kept well out of harm's way.

Even birds that were hundreds of miles away, whilst migrating south to South Florida, took shelter well before the hurricanes struck. They did not continue their journey south until the storms had passed and it was safe to fly to their intended destinations. As a rule, birds do not require maps or weather forecasts by meteorologists. They trust their inbuilt natural powers that nature has always provided for them since their first flights on earth many moons ago.

Perhaps, because human beings have evolved with extra mental sophistication, filling their minds full of bookish information, they have inadvertently paid a big price. There is little doubt contemporary humans have diminished their natural, instinctive animal awareness to nature's dangers, in comparison to all other animals.

Many serious accidents that kill or maim people present themselves on a daily basis. Mostly they result from a lack of attention to the surrounding environment or situation. For instance, a moment of distraction driving a motor car at seventy miles an hour can cause a major pile up with the deaths of many involved. Skiing off piste can end-up in disaster, because the skier did not heed the dangers involved. Building houses at the edge of cliffs or in areas that are low lying or living in trailer parks in hurricane prone areas are disasters waiting to happen. The catalogue of unresponsiveness to nature's perils is proficiently recorded in the history books and persists unabated.

There are numerous situations and actions humans continue to perform from moment-to-moment ... All can be classed as accidents waiting to happen ... Its just a matter of when!

Even everyday habits such as smoking or eating unhealthy foods continue as hazardous practices for many people. However, in these cases it is not out of ignorance of the dangers humans suffer but in-spite of them. No other animals on earth would willingly put their lives at risk by following human being's foolish lifestyles, even if they could. Their ingrained invisible strengths would signal danger and they would find greener pastures to graze.

Thankfully, humans do still possess some connection to animal awareness, for when all is said and done; the human races are still animals. Human responsiveness to alchemy forces is viewable in many sports venues. For example, when a golfer is in a 'purple patch' he can put the ball in the hole from incredible places on the green or even from the fairway. None can explain what is happening, but all know something is at work that takes the game to a higher level beyond the ordinary. They sense an ecstasy and ball control greater than any way they normally know-how.

There is little doubt when success is concerned; human awareness of divine chemistry used every day. Maybe it is in different ways than nature intended; nevertheless, thanks to the media we see it everywhere. In the business arena, on the stock market, acting, singing, painting or writing, everybody, at one time in their lives, will experience a 'purple patch' when everything goes way outside their normal expectations. For a few, it repeats itself throughout a lifetime. For the majority, it is just a flash-in-the-pan.

However, it is possible that because people use their invisible powers to enhance their skills in an unnatural, fabricated environment, they have lost their intrinsic, natural awareness of nature. It seems humanity in general, has misplaced, a large allocation of the natural instincts that alerts a person to dangers and natural disasters. Maybe there would be far fewer deaths from nature's disasters if human beings could relocate that simple natural package of awareness they embraced when mortals took their first steps on earth.

Before the launch of the next rocket to outer space by 'brilliant' scientists, the question that demands an answer is ... How much better-off and happier are human beings today compared to our animal brethren, who still retain all their unsophisticated, unadulterated natural powers?

Oscars for Shadows

Staid lives pass-by, mostly unnoticed,
occasionally, there may be a soiree
on the terrace of ambitions,
friends and family
will applaud and cheer, feed the ego,
for a few irresistible moments,
but, on the whole,
a life will sail past, furbished in hush,
nobody will notice its golden interior,
illuminated in elegant ingenious creativity,
time expires in modest silence,
a few vivid shadows may
be vocalized
in lament,
as the picture book pages turn.

The Icing on the Cake

A little girl was watching her mum make her favorite cake. It was filled with lots of nuts and fruit and the top had pink icing. After a few minutes, the little girl asked her mum if she would bake her cake with just the yummy pink icing, because that was her favorite part of the cake. Her mother told her child that all the ingredients that are good for her are inside the cake, not on the surface. She went on to tell her that the icing on top sure tastes nice, but consuming only the icing would make her very sick indeed.

She elaborated, as we journey through life many temptations, luxury items and expensive lifestyles, are introduced to us, via the advertising media. Acquiring many extravagant possessions and lavish things that seem very enjoyable, becomes the goal of most ambitious, aspiring people ... Sure enough, when people set their goals and are persistent in their pursuit of their materialistic dreams, they will achieve material wealth.

However; it has been my experience in meeting many wealthy people who have over indulged in life's luxuries, be it ... Too much refined food, too much alcohol, too much worry over investments etc, etc,... They have ruined their health and would give it all up to regain the vigor and energy they had when they were young, health and ambitious.

When they were indulging in all the goodies and everything seemed to be going their way, they would declare... "I want to live as I want to live and no-one will tell me otherwise."
However; when the moment of truth arrived and they were staring death in the face, after many years of suffering a prolonged illness ...They would say... "If Only I have taken more care of myself and not been guided by my foolish ego"

They all forgot where the good ingredients were stored in their life and settled for the sweet tastes of what they deemed success. This brought them ample helpings of icing on the cake, but it also meant they were too full to partake in all the really healthy components that add up to a truly prosperous life. It also signified true happiness was in very short supply.

Moderation in all things is the key to true health, wealth and happiness. It is very rewarding to harvest the fruits of our labor and acquiring great wealth is fine, just so long as we all realize it is only a superficial, outward appearance and no-thing can make up for genuine love & joy...For without those two authentic ingredients, no amount of money will make us happy.

Love and Joy are not tangible assets, but we all possess them... In true reality, they are our only real, eternal possessions... In fact, they are not even possessions at all, for the infinite quantum energy of love & joy is all we are, once we strip away all the icing on the cake (materialism in all forms), The good news is our indisputable essence of energy will go on forever, no matter how we abuse our bodies.... However, isn't it so much better to enjoy our true selves (love& joy) whilst we have the mind and body to do so. As the famous bard William Shakespeare once said..."To thy own self be true"

When mother finished baking the cake and relating her wisdom, the little girl asked if she would be as good a cake maker when she grows up. Her very wise mum replied, "When you learn what can be produced in only seven days (figuratively speaking), you will know nothing is impossible.

You have your whole life in front of you my precious darling and you can achieve whatever you set your mind to as long as it embodies good intent.... All your dreams and aspirations will manifest themselves for the benefit and prosperity of humanity. The more you help others, the more you will progress. Allow your guide to be the intelligence that created you, then your life on earth will be lived in a state of stress-free grace and kindness.... Just don't be consumed by too much icing... It is not education that breeds success; rather, it is the success in the breed ...That educates others

A Place to Live

Rivers of wisdom stream into infinities imaginations,

Flow into the minds of empty slumbering silence,

Blooms of love flourishing on trees of joy,

Seeds of contentment sown in tranquil hearts,

What a beautiful place to spend the rest of our lives.

The Course Will Close Itself

All golf cubs must abide by the rules of golf that are laid down by The Royal and Ancient rulebook. I remember a debate that raged in Manchester, UK some twenty years ago. The question was when the golf course should be closed by inclement weather. The debate went on for many years, as many members did not take kindly to the whims of the green keeper, the golf pro or the different captains the club had each year. Then a wise man came up with a suggestion...Let the course close itself. If the weather is so bad that the cups fill with water and the greens become water logged, then it becomes impossible to play golf. If there is a snow blizzard, how can anyone hit a golf ball and find it... So naturally, the course will close itself. This settled all the debates and so it came to pass a local rule passed... Nature would decide if the course was playable. The course would close itself.

If we live our lives according to the laws of nature, we will live a healthy, prosperous life. The big problem in today's world is there is a big debate going on:
• What is healthy?
• What is unhealthy?
• What causes dis-ease?
• What is the source of happiness?
• What will elevate stress?
• What will eliminate stress?
• What foods nourish the mind & body?
• What foods destroy the mind & body?

Frequently, scientific research is performed and the results often conflict with a pervious study done by another group. I guess it all depends on who is funding the study as to what the results will reveal. Commercial or political parties, who have self-interest in the results, fund many studies and therefore they are unreliable. It is not much fun to find out you have been eating the wrong foods, for say ten years, because a famous doctor announced they would be good for you. In all sincerity, perhaps he thought the food would be good nourishment conveying good health, but it is, at best, just one person's, or one group's opinion and opinions can and do distort the truth.

"Happiness is nothing more than good health and a bad memory." - Albert Schweitzer:

As science advances, it will no doubt find new methods of fixing up diseased bodies. It will also come up with new formulas to keep healthy, but why do we need new formulas when the simple wise and wholesome formulas work so well...What are they...Lets explore!

How about we bring in a new local rule, which is as old as the hills.... 'The mind and body will dictate what foods we eat and what thought we think." That seems simple enough does it not? It is simple, but it is so obvious that most people ignore it.

• If you eat a food that gives you indigestion, you are eating foods, which your body does not appreciate. Perhaps you are eating too quickly, or you are in a stressful situation.
• If you are overweight, you are eating too much food. Most probably, it is high in fat or sugar.
• If you are not sleeping well there are events in your life you find difficult to deal with.

The mind and body are united by a very complex and fascinating system. The human mind and body is a whole universe unto itself. I will not go into details about the fantastic systems humans have because I do not know how it all works within scientific details... But I do know how to listen-in to it and keep healthy with the aid of universal, intelligent wisdom.

"If you are distressed by anything external, the pain is not due to the thing itself, but to your estimate of it; and this you have the power to revoke at any moment." _ Marcus Aurelius.

The mind connects to the immune system, and it is in the gut that the immune system obtains much of its information. You could say the gut and the mind work in conjunction with each other to regulate the well being of every cell in its body. Indeed, every cell is a universe unto itself and it accepts it has to work together with all the other cells in the body to function as nature intended...If there is a mis-communication in the mind and body bond, certain functions would close down.

The course of principled, reciprocating actions will close itself down when the ego/intellect interferes with the universal circuitry, thanks to erroneous thought patterns. If the mis-communication carries on for a long period, more and more cells of the body will close down until eventually the whole system goes haywire and death is the final game played. The course of the mind and body has closed itself prematurely, ahead of its assigned, natural lifetime on earth. Stymied by a conditioned mind, filled with fabricated opinions, assumptions and theories, that does not conform to nature.

The circuitry of the human body is an incredible computer programmed by the texture and fabric of nature. The main communicator between the mind and the gut is the vagus nerve, derived from the Latin word which means to wander. The mind wanders into the domain of the gut and likewise, the gut wanders into domain of the mind.

Without exception, every cell in a human mind and body reflects in concert and they conduct in synchronicity with each other. The conscious mind decides what foods to put into the gut. The gut will send a message back if it does not like what the mind is shoving in it.

They will both work to fix any malfunction, however if one small part of the brain, namely the taste buds dictates what is to be consumed and digested, it can wreak havoc and devastation in your magnificent universal system. The memory-banks are programmed to spark tastes that require high fat and sugar and once programmed, they become the reference points when the stomach sends its hungry signals.

"The mind is its own place, and in itself, can make heaven of Hell, and a hell of Heaven." - John Milton.

To overcome past conditioning of harmful foods and thoughts a new identity is required that transcends programmed memories. By listening into the signals from the divine alchemist philosopher in the gut, a new regime of eating can yield amazing results in just a few weeks. Simply put....Just eat what your stomach requires...Just think thoughts that do not churn it.....Just enjoy natures bounty of wholesome foods and simple thoughts and observe how your miraculous universal body aligns with every star in the sky.

The course of original nature will be open for you to follow all your life on earth...As you plant your thoughts, so shall you harvest the fruits of happiness. The biorhythms of genuine health are naturally orchestrated, in every cell of your body and mind. Tune-into the guts, alchemy wise, authentic intelligence... Observes how you magically transform your life-journey into an open, trustworthy, live alchemy course. Ever changing, into higher realms of divine bliss.

Sounds of My Life...From People Around the World

The sound of a contented cats purr... enchanting music to my ears,

A shrieks of the modem.... instantly connecting me to the world of the Internet,

The hummingbirds who visit me ... heavenly hums, soul to soul,

A voice of a frog that is not aware that I am here... I rejoiced with him,

The wind chimes on my patio.... mystical trees sway in Synchronicity,

As a Crickets chirps... silence stars shine through my old oak trees,

The soft delicate breath of my... angelic sleeping children,

A family happily chomping together at meal times... my cooking, my pleasure,

The tick-tock of the grandfather clock... reminds me of my newborn baby's future,

A Rhapsody in Blue... Played by my insightful child prodigy,

The magical sound shhhh... listen to my 100 year old mother's wisdom,

A whistle of my tea kettle... on an icy winter's morn,

The buzz of the bees... honey spread on crisp whole-wheat toast,

A playful clarinet accompanying a celestial violin... The applause of a standing ovation.

The symphony of my nature... Words of divine kindness,

The sound of easy music blending with a bird's song... as rain drops on the window,

The crisp spring evenings precious sound... moonlight over my awesome ocean,

A sound of one moment and the next... and the next... and the next.

The delicate sound of my inner voice...smoothing out my behavior over the mayhem and chaos,

A beloved's heartbeat... entwined in my devoted embrace,

The snoring old beloved in my bed...my mate for sixty years,

The voice my love conducts... the creators alchemy orchestrations,

The last words spoken, from my dearly departed mate... "I love you"
The many sounds of my life... With love & happiness - I witness it all, and give thanks to the mystical conductor.

Divorcing Emotions from Feelings

The End of a Marriage Controlled By Ignorance
There are many fine books written on stress management and self help systems to heal emotional wounds. If these systems work so well, why are the same people continually buying more books and paying for more seminars? Surely if the philosophy they are reading works, it will continue to work in all circumstances and not just deal with their current problems.

Most negative emotions become habit forming so that when we anger or hate, we do so automatically without having to think about it. Likewise, with worry and anxiety, we become auto-trained to look for the negative in our daily lives.

One good example: reading the morning newspaper that we know is crammed with sensationalist reporting that embellishes events worse than they are. Still, we read the similar style negative news each day. I know we cannot help being concerned about all the horrific things happening in our world, but fretting and worrying solves nothing and only contributes to a pathway to a hospital bed.

Perhaps you no longer read the newspapers now, but still feel wound up with close relatives or friends. You could be in a problematic marriage or have a child on drugs. It could be, you suffer aged parents that need constant attention... Maybe the boss gives you a hard time, or maybe it is some other work colleague, who is striving to climb the corporate ladder before you do... Many situations can cause stress and strains that will produce a lethargic and listless disposition, eventually resulting in a severe disorder of the mind and body .

Subsequently, what are we to do... just learn to manage our stress levels, or can we mostly eliminate emotional stress? I say mostly because there are always going to be situations that surprise us and we may revert to our old reference points in our minds for a short period. Therefore, we require starting out with a commitment for change. A new focus and thought process with fresh, wise, mindful reference points are required to formulate a new lifestyle emotionally free of all negativity.

The first step is to become aware we are functioning with an auto-emotional-response-system on a continuing basis. Any sign of disagreement from someone and we will respond in anger. Anything goes wrong and we immediately start to worry. We have to realize that many events we will face in our lifetime are making us react in an emotional manner without thinking things through first. A self-awareness of our complete lack of control, of our aggressive behavior and our negative assertive manner is essential to begin our approach to a stress free life. We need to recognize, we are being governed by outside events and other peoples opinions, rather than our own inner intelligence system.

"We choose our joys and sorrows long before we experience them." - Kahlil Gibran.

Once we become aware of our adverse emotional actions and reactions, we can commence to find the cause of our emotional effects. We will begin to realize that our minds have been accustomed to think in a certain way that is normal by most people's standards, but is very much distance from anything natural. Many well meaning 'Gurus' will tell us we need to feel other people's pain before we can understand our own. As if our own pain is not bad enough, we have to pile other people's problems into our mind and feel their pain... What poppycock!

Yes, we need to feel empathy towards our fellow brothers and sisters and understand their pain, but to feel their pain on top of our own uncontrollable sentiments will certainly add to our emotional baggage. Why encourage other people's negativity when we cannot deal with our own. We have to get our own house in order before we can teach others to purify their house.

Therefore, after a period of self-refection and close emotional scrutiny, we now realize we have a problem with many uncontrollable sensations that knots up our stomach. Stirrings that cause us aggravating worry and uncontrollable anger, that drain us of positive energy.

This is where I become controversial and fly-in-the-face of most psychologists and so called 'experts' on emotional behavior. If we keep on following 'band-aid' medication remedies, eventually the band-aid will not work anymore, for the festering underneath the band-aid, will become life threatening.

Everything you are experiencing in your emotional roller coaster of a life is an illusion... Some experts may exclaim that statement is nonsense. Perhaps so, I may be regarded as strange, from some psychotherapists' quarters, but I am not the one suffering from any negative emotions and maybe some of the psycho-experts are?

Yes... yes... a thousand times yes. All negative emotions are illusionary figments, which signal depressing images to an overactive, inventive ego/personality, disciplined to react.

Thousands of years of DNA evolution has programmed our bodies to react to an emotional state of mind. Of courses, life was a lot tougher thousands of years ago and there was a need for swift actions to escape dangerous situations. However, if we fretted and were scared or angered beyond control, we probably would not have been able to defend ourselves properly and would have swiftly perished to a predator. As we progressed and led more sedate lives, our negative emotions increased and our ability to respond in the correct manner to danger decreased.

Today we are at the point of no return, for there are no real answers coming from the experts to eliminate negative emotions. They just tell us the best we can do is to manage stress with meditation, exercise and a good diet...In addition, in some extreme cases - strong medication.

Some studies have shown when we experience a lot of stress, arteries can harden and excessive exercise is the last thing we should do, as it could be fatal. The learning and wisdom within our higher alchemy self, is far more important in our daily lives, than anything else we should learn at collage. If we are living life with a personality/ego that is not genuinely human in the traditional authentic sense, how can we live as true human beings?

"It is impossible for a man to learn what he thinks he already knows." - Epictetus.

Now we come to the crux of the matter. We are not living life as human beings anymore. We are living as a programmed set of emotions, redesigned to react to stressful situations. If we have the wrong identity, it is obvious the only thing we can do is make the best of a bad job. Moreover, that means we can only manage stress and not eliminate it. Before we can progress, we have to redefine the dictionary. Since we only have a limited vocabulary to work with, we need to find new meanings for old words so we can understand how to advance and live a stress free life.

"You cannot step twice into the same river, for other waters are continually flowing in." - Heraclitus.

Let's take the words "emotions' and "feelings':
Emotion is linked with the word feeling in every dictionary and embraces

love, hate, fear, worry, joy, etc., under the same umbrella. The negatives link with the positives in both of the words, emotion and feelings. What if we divorced the two words, from each other?

Separate meanings and separate lives.

They are no longer compatible partners so a wise judge has detached them. They should never have been married in the first place, as it was a mismatch fashioned in Hell by an ignorant intellect that could not find a word to separate a curse from a virtue. Love and hate have opposite effects on our mind and bodies so how can they live compatibly together in one word?

"Some men see things as they are and say, "Why?" I dream of things that never were and say, "Why not?" _ George Bernard Shaw.

Let's use the word emotion to describe all the negative stuff and let's use the word feeling for love and joy and all that positive energy that stems from it. 'Emotion' is going off to live a life of torment, while 'feelings' is going to live a life of bliss. After all, why should feelings suffer at emotions expense? They should never have formed a union in the first place. Now is the time to rectify an epoch of turmoil and disorder.

So, on one hand we have the emotions that cause grief and heartbreak (in both senses) Then we have feelings that contain love, joy and all the beautiful wonders that stem from such radiant blooms.

Feelings are also part of our senses (to feel) whereas emotions are not one of the five senses of taste, smell, see, hear, and touch. The last sense 'touch' means 'to feel', so when we love and live in joy we can feel it in every molecule of our body once our neurons receive the 'feelings' signal.

The best the uncontrollable emotions can accomplish is to feed messages of distress from observing actions and events, which contain no love or joy - just negativity.

If we comprehend that, our time on earth is limited to 75 years on average, why waste time pandering to the demands of the emotions when we have the veracious, dependable, blissful feelings to replace the negativity.

If a person starts to use verbal abusive language in our direction, we see s/he is under the clutches of negative emotions, so we contact our authentic feelings and send them our love and joy. We have replaced our old way of reacting, with a new way of dealing with negative emotions. Rather than giving in to another person's emotions, that may harm us, we strengthen the proactive response, by the inner live alchemy of love and joy. It was here within us all the time. We have now rediscovered it exists. It is like learning to walk and talk all over again.

But what about the death of a loved one? What about events such as 9/11? Surely, we cannot be emotionless about such catastrophic events. This is the big challenge we all face, for we will experience the death of our beloved ones at some time. It is at this point in our lives that we need to be psychologically prepared and this is where our new training is an indispensable requirement. A deeper understanding of love and joy is now required. They are more than just feelings in the sense we have described so far.

'Love and joy' is an energy force that controls everything in our world. It is the quantum glue that binds all life forms. 'Love and joy' is part of Spirit's power, dwelling in our bodies and we recognize it as a Soul. We need to grasp we are the Soul, we are the energy, we are the life force labeled Soul. In this state of mind, the human alchemy can perform its magical changes for the betterment of humanity.

The Love and Joy of the Soul is intelligent energy that transfuses life with the reasons to exist. That is why these feelings transcend all else. They are spirits/universal intelligence's, personal way of contacting physical beings.

If we lose love and joy, we lose the reason to live. We lose or contact with our maker, our mentor, our maestro. Who or what can direct our orchestrations if we have no conductor? We will be out of tune and out of compositions.

Without Spirits guiding light, we are depressed and lack love and joy. Our immune system starts to lose strength to protect us and we eventually die of dis-ease. We decompose physically far too soon.

The Soul (love and joy) cannot die, therefore even though disaster has struck our personal world, we still have the power of spirit's love and joy to feel and bathe in.

"All things change; nothing perishes." _ Ovid.

The beloved who has physically died continues to be sensed within the heart, through our love infused joy, conveying sunshine where storm clouds have gathered. Yes, we will miss the physical contacts of kisses and hugs, but eventually all people physically die and since it is an undeniable event, we should not feel any sorrow, but we do.

Well, how can we feel sorrow, when we have divorced those negative emotions to where they belong - to the world of fiction and illusions that is required by a personality that does not know its own Identity. Do you really want to try and patch things up with your emotions and remarry them to your feelings - well, do you?

"I am always doing that which I can not do, in order that I may learn how to do it."_ Pablo Picasso

I know this way of thinking may seem quite strange at first. Many intellectual people will ridicule it and say, emotions and feelings, cannot be separated - that is just the way it is. Well, for those folks, that is the way it is and always will be whilst they are on earth. But now, you have more choices to make. You can continue as 'normal' people do and live life on an emotional rollercoaster or you can embrace your feelings, as 'natural' people will. Your love and joy is your personal connection to Spirit's truth. Do you want to live a prosperous life with your feelings? Do you really have any 'real' choice?

"All truth passes through three stages: first, it is ridiculed; next it is violently attacked; finally, it is held to be self-evident." - Schopenhauer

Free Will

The ocean; she pays no mind...no heed to herself,
She allows herself to wander freely,
To evaporate from sight,
then; to appear in the sky
as free forming, towering clouds
any shape _ stratospheric ...any size _ translucent
black, white and all shades in-between,
To wonder where she may,
night or day,
Wonder freely across mountains,
across valleys...across dales,
And ; The ocean...she cares not,
For she has no worries, no woes,

84

Because; the ocean knows that all......
All that evaporates and travels far....far away,
will one day return home and be content,
To tell of sublime tales...of noble adventures,
that blew them off course,
thrust by hurricanes and mighty winds,
unleashing such monumental power,
gargantuan bolts of sound,
 awesome streaking light,
The magnificent view they had,
of all natures scenery,
as the metamorphism,
reversed itself once again,
transformed as lucid raindrops,
into streams, ponds, lakes,
seeping into earths crust,
flowing into raging rivers,
then finally
Back home
flowing;
In the rhythm of time.

The Whys in the Road?

Each day in our lives there are decisions to be made. Most are small but nevertheless can have significant impact on our happiness. We amble along and make the most of each situation we face as the result of our actions. But there will come a time when we come to a BIG fork in the road ... A big Y.
Do we turn left or right?

Perhaps we have been laid off from a job we had for twenty years or more? Maybe we are confronting a divorce after twenty years of matrimony or was it purgatory?

Possibly we are grieving after the tragic death of a loved one for whom we cared and nurtured for many loving years?

Perhaps we are 'worried sick' about a war with Iraq and all the ramifications from other countries.

Could our sick stock portfolio be a reason we are visiting the doctor?

Maybe we've been diagnosed with a debilitating illness.

Which road are we to follow now and where will it take us?
How do we make our decisions?
To whom do we listen?
Do we take the advice of a good friend who means well, but has not grasped true meaning in their life?
 Do we take the counsel of our doctor who has not found the cure or the reason for his own illness?
Should we listen to our accountant, lawyer or broker, who could have a host of corporations giving them commission for all the clients they send?
Who is it we can trust?

The road ahead has many twists and turns. Even if we choose the correct route, why then, many diversions and detours will be placed in our way. And should we choose the wrong route, why then, we will only get lost at many junctions which will take us deeper into the abyss of a nomadic erratic life. Many why's to ponder.

86

The biggest being
Why Me?
Why is life treating ME so cruelly?
What have I done to deserve this?

The answers are as complex as the life we fabricate. If we have fabricated
a life of little meaning, then ... Why-becomes-Because. We have traveled
routes that were enjoyable when our journey started but became boring or
monotonous as it wound its way round each bend in the road. Many times,
we stopped short. We did not go the extra mile.
We forgot to tell our loved ones how much we loved them every day.
We forgot to pleasingly complete the job in hand at work, which would
have given an outstanding result instead of just a good result.
We forgot to forgive a relative or friend and now they are gone forever.
We ignored the warning signs our body was telling us and carried on
regardless of stressful symptoms.
We ignored the warning signs the stock market was telling us. Fear and
greed ruled. Then, all of a sudden ... `Too late be the cry.' Could these be a
few of the reasons to the question why?

There are probably enough Whys in our lives to put us in a state of
depression for a long and unhappy time and then end up dying of some
incurable dis-ease.
One of the oldest adages is "as you sow so shall you reap."

Now many times we will say I have always thought good thoughts about
folks and I have always done what it is that was expected of me. But
expected by whom, other folks who are asking why? Could it be a case of
the blind leading the blind into a fabricated life that is man made and has
lost Universal guidance. Are we so intent in pleasing a misguided society
that we go down the wrong route even though our instinct and intuition are
telling us `No don't go that way.'

Could it be we have taken the wrong fork in the road many years ago, and
now we are just realizing we are back at the crossroads? Perhaps we were
at the crossroads many years ago but our minds, we were so fogged up by
polluted thoughts, we drove into a future crisis, with no map to find our
way out.

You will hear many people say life is a struggle. Life is an endurance test.
We have to suffer to gain heavenly bliss. These jumbled-up thoughts were
handed-down to people, generation after generation, for thousands of

years. Now many believe this to be our truth. That is why we are at the fork in the road and do not know which way to go.

Our Whys have no answer, for when we say; "that is how it is. It is destiny. It is fate. It is impossible to be in Joy all the time."

For all the folks who think this way, why then, that is how it is. So they will continue to say Why me, and never will they come close to a significant answer. Not until the `Why Me' tune into the `Real Me's route to happiness. When we begin to follow wisdom's blueprint of the super infinite highway all is unburdened. Only then will we find the correct route in the Y's of life.

The Whys, within the crossroads, which lead to wisdom's intelligence of boundless thoroughfares to joy.
It takes many years of practice to obtain anything close to perfection. In Spirit, there are No choices, No freewill, No Why's in the road. There is only perfection, with an infinite truthfulness of dimensions of divine bliss. When we progress down life's path with the wisdom of universal intelligence as our guide, we find we ride the on a first class ticket, luxuriously surrounded by mother earths richness.

We find wellness is an absence of illness and we live well.

Financially, wealth finds its way to us. We do not need to chase after it. We magnetize everything we need by understanding we need very little to enjoy life.
And there lays the secret... We need to enjoy living life as a servant of spirit and not try to be its master.
Why? ...Why, then we find it is impossible not to be in JOY 24 hours a day.
Every day-in, every way … And it gets better all the time.
It is the only true free-way to prosperity.
Time to encompass; The Real "Me."... Our True, Ageless, Unrestrained Soul.

Hush Little Child

Hush little child,
whimpering in dreams,
you're all cozy and warm,
wrapped in rainbows and moonbeams,
outside the wind howls,
there's frost on the ground,
and Autumn is whining,
its early warning sound,
so hush my baby,
there's no cause for alarm,
for in your life,
you'll face many a storm,
But with God at your side,
there is nothing to fear,
Because spirits love and affection,
will always be near.

The Drill Sergeant

The Drill Sergeant calls parade and all the troops' line up preparing for our birth. The main commands are attention, present arms, quick march, halt, and at ease. We are born ...What a wondrous world to arrive and play role games, for a few moments in time .

When we come into the world we are at ease with life, we enter as an innocent baby and have no preconceived ideas of what we want to do or what type of personality we will adopt. We do have a DNA, which will shape our lives and mold our character to a certain extent. We have joy, love and free will to embrace the world with happy innocence. We have the power to observe and learn, as our minds take notes of the actions of the people that surround our space on earth. We have started our preliminary training.

At seven years of age, it is time to en-role. Time to start playing our serious roles, formed from the ego that is fabricated in our conscious minds. Up to this point, most of us were allowed the freedom of childhood, but it was within an indoctrination of a great multitude of negative thoughts. All these thoughts attach themselves to the personality we build. Once we enlist in society's doctrines and regulations, we have to go on parade and learn the drill on how to implement them.

We have many sergeants to teach us how to obey the commands of the generals. Our parents, relations, friends, teachers, religious leaders and media folks, will each in turn, put us into training. Our subconscious minds will learn how to obey orders without questioning them for their authenticity. Our commanders, were also taught by their sergeant's when they were children, so they have learned the commands well and automatically teach the same erroneous stuff.

The roles we are to play out in our lives are about to take shape.
Boss or worker.
Friend or foe.
Which religious group to follow.
Which banner to hold?
Which academic decoration to hide behind.
Which labels to stick on our image?
Which emotions are being trained to auto-over-react to each situation that we will face on a daily basis?

None are real, just man made images. But we must learn the drill until we conform and they become reality.

We first learn to form a line. To line up with all the other recruits. We must all conform to the rules and regulations of unsound emotions. The first command is Attention. We have to become ridged on command, "At - tension." Our first lesson is to learn how to become tense and stop our merriment. We soon learn that if we don't obey this command we will suffer the consequences and be punished by the rule makers. Smiling and laughing too much will not be tolerated.

Our at-tension must be programmed to hold tension. This becomes our normality after a few practice drills. The few people that don't comply have many sergeants chasing after them shouting at them to fall in line with everybody else. Most peoples smile diminish, for this training is very thorough..... Each and every person must be rounded up into the herd mentality of negative emotions.

Once we learn the tension bit, we are taught to present arms. To show we have weapons to fight with and kill if necessary. We must take care of our weapons and make sure they are in working order. Revenge, spite, hatred, jealousy, fear, trepidation and a myriad of other dark negatives, all begin to manifest in our mind. All are silent killers and one day will backfire on the holder, deteriorating into diseased cells of the body

The next command is "quick march"... We are learning to march off into conflicts and fights with other humans for whatever reason are around at that moment-in-time. All the reasons will connect to holding on to or obtaining a possession or image of some kind. Even if the possession is our own self-image, political viewpoint or religion, it will be worth fighting over by the reasoning and logic of the disciplined, unfavorable emotions.

We have now learnt to march through life at-tension. We can look around and occasionally glance at the beauty and virtues of humanity. Maybe go on a short holiday for a couple of weeks but as soon as we get back, we must recommence our quick march through life and hold tension. When we have marched long enough the commander shrieks "Halt" ... We have developed an illness and can no longer run with the herd. We were not allowed to stop until this instruction was given. We are told to form a line and then the command "at ease" is given. We are now allowed to ease this tension by medications or surgery.... However, we are still in line. At this stage of the game, the illness is not life threatening, so we can continue as though nothing has happened, for we can rely on doctors and medication for our well-being.

By following our society and culture, we have learned all the negative ways of thinking that bring tension into our lives. Our attention was focused on obtain materialist wants, to enhance our lifestyle. Marching off to work each day to fight with the competition or with he boss, climbing the mountains of worries involved with modern day living. We had many people around, instructing us that this is the proper 'normal' way to live. They give us the thoughts, encouraging us to battle with others, to achieve our goals.

Grasping and grabbing our slice of the action and driven on by our own internal drill sergeant within our conditioned mind that is working over-time, on autopilot. More and tenser feelings build-up, then one day a bellowing loud voice shouts "Halt." Devastation has occurred. We realize life has passed us by and although we may have achieved our goal of wealth, our march was in vain for we have no joy. We become sicker and frailer and die without knowing how to live at real ease...To make life real easy.

If the "halt" command comes soon enough, from an authentic source, we had at birth... Then we can follow another more authentic route to find the ease, without having to be commanded by doctors to ease. However, if we only have to rely on the orders to ease by doctors' prescriptions, then this means we still adhere to the whims of other mis-conditioned human beings, for most doctors will also die of a disease. If they can't help themselves then how can they help others? ..... This then is a false "at ease," because we can relax, but only in the confines of our own negative conditioned mind and kept alive by medication. This ease is only temporary and in fact it is not "real ease" for the mind is still troubled and the cause of illness hidden.

"A real ease" releases us from the constrictions of a negative mind. Just seeing ourselves as only flesh and blood will never allow us to be "at ease" in this "normal' world. The physical seems real enough but it does not last and we worry when it does not perform as we think it should. If we have to wait for a doctor to tell us to slow down then we have already missed a large chunk of our lives.

We do not need modern society's erroneous thinking, filled with media hype, to drill us on the way to live our lives, it does not work and only leads to a life of tensions. There is a better way...De-list from the thinking that has contributed to an early grave or an unfulfilled life for many people. Refuse to become immersed in society's normality and live naturally, as nature intended. If you want to learn how...Then observe how a dog gives unconditioned love to others. It is that simple.

The universal law of good intent is a golden rule that cannot be broken by any drill sergeant commands. If we treat others, as we would like to be treated, then we live as natural human beings... Only then, will the 'normal' negative life drills, march far, far away, to the beat of the erroneous, dogmatic drummer.

The Man from Nowhere
The mask slips - as the doors close,
time to undertake - an invisible Pose
a man from nowhere - who nobody knows,
obscure and aloof - from society's shows.

The nameless one - no symbol or label,
all the cards laid bare - on the banquet table,
blowing in the wind - that once rocked his cradle,
a prince among men - now only a fable.

A statue standing - in the town square,
people come - to gaze and stare,
they look for a second - but really don't care,
about the lonely figure of the man from nowhere.

An icon to the world - now fertile as the land,
quietly drifts through time - a solitary grain of sand,
echo wisps of voice - eerie ghostly command,
the man from nowhere - no longer in demand.

Part Three - The Masterpiece, The Joy of Live Alchemy

As Real As a Rainbow

As we gaze out on the horizon twixt ocean and sky, we can sometimes observe a magnificent rainbow arching over the waves. It is indeed a spectacular sight, but how real is it? A rainbow is made up from seven colors Red, Blue, Yellow, Green, Orange, Indigo, Violet and when we add Black and White, we have the paint box that colors every-thing on earth. The rays of sunlight enters a rain droplet and then the pure white light is reflected inside the prism of the raindrop then split into seven colors which we refer to as the spectrum..... A wave band of exotic vivid air. That in itself is a miraculous reflection of imagination for none of it is tangible to human touch, taste, smell or hearing...... it can only be viewed through the lens of human eyesight

Descartes first thought about the construction of a rainbow, by viewing it as, one single drop of water and how it interacts with sunlight. He wrote; "Considering that this bow appears not only in the sky, but also in the air near us, whenever there are drops of water illuminated by the sun, as we can see in certain fountains. I readily decided that it arose only from the way in which the rays of light act on these drops and pass from them to our eyes. Further, knowing that the drops are round, as has been formerly proved, and seeing that whether they are larger or smaller, the appearance of the bow is not changed in any way, I had the idea of making a very large one, so that I could examine it better."

A little later in time a scientist by the name of Isaac Newton discovered that by shining a beam of sunlight through a glass prism it split into the seven colors of the rainbow. The question is how real is color and then the question becomes ... How real is real?

Just as a rainbow appears in the sky and vanishes just as quickly, so human life on earth sparks in a flash, as the sperm enters the egg. Life also finishes just as abruptly with the expiration of life's energizing vitality.

The interlude between life and death is but a star-twinkle in cosmic terms. So, is a human life on earth just a well fashioned rainbow that seems real enough, but is, in true essence, just a reflection of cosmic particles that project animated objects that contain universal intelligence. Indeed, comparing humans with a rainbow... it must be as intelligent as a human or how else could it form itself in the same immaculate shape and color order every time?

Of course, some intellects will state, just automated, mechanical nature gives a rainbow its form. However, all of nature needs an orchestration and no orchestration can be in-tune without a conductor. How different is the reality of a rainbow to the reality of a human life, bearing in mind most of the human body was once a rainbow shining in the sky. (The human body is over eighty percent water). Just because we have a brain with intellectual knowledge, it does not mean we can be any more real than a rainbow. Worry and anxiety manifest from a mind that is out of tune with its own identity/selfhood.

The bottom line is, we can all live as beaming, colorful, human rainbows. Therefore, how about we shine our radiance throughout humanity, to develop into the authentic beacons of light we were intended to be. Rainbows don't make wars and never worry about the outlook, for they discern that after every storm they will refresh and renew within a clouds silver lining.

The next time you see a rainbow in the sky remember... You are looking at the future generations of humanity in a more colorful light...

I Am The One

I am the discreet whispers, on the breeze.
Listen to my voice, as it brushes your delicate cheek,
I am within, all you think, all you seem, all you contemplate,
My thoughts etched, in every rock

Through eons of years, I have called your name,
no replies heard, no true purpose found,
Listen to my voice, as it sails upon the wind,
Be on familiar terms with my message,
to uncover authentic meaning.

As I float on by your mind, be aware,
You know I am around you,
Yet you will not listen to my voice
Could it be your choice,
is not of your souls choosing?

I am, your own true-self, dear one,
I give birth to forever and a day,
Will you suffer, in your illusions,
endure rather than enjoy,
or will you becalm your mind,
become aware, of my timeless silent voice,

The Treasure Hunt

I remember a story I was told when I was knee high to a grasshopper...
A man is searching for a valuable coin he dropped in the street.
Another man is passing-by and asks; "can I help you."
"That is very kind of you, yes, please help me look for the coin I dropped."
"When did you drop it?"
"About four hours ago"
"Humm? Did you drop it in this exact location?"
"Well; No, I dropped it around the corner"
"So why are you looking for it here?"
"It is very dark around the corner and the street lights
are so much brighter in this part of the street!"

"Education is an admirable thing, but it is well to remember from time to
time that nothing that is worth knowing can be taught."
-Oscar Wilde

How many times do we do things in our life because the bright, educated
experts say that is the correct thing to do?

Doctors, lawyers, professors, financial advisers, politicians, religious
leaders etc, etc, etc, could all be well meaning folks, who may give us
intellectual advice they have studied at university. Indeed some of it may
be good advice, but a great deal of it may not. In fact, it could dispatch us
down a path of ruination and havoc.

"I have learnt silence from the talkative, toleration from the intolerant, and
kindness from the unkind; yet strangely, I am ungrateful to these
teachers."- Kahlil Gibran

Just because a person has educational qualifications does not mean they
know how to live an authentic life on earth.

•• If doctors develop an illness and die from a disease, how can they
prevent their patients from getting a disease? The best cure from illness is
prevention of illness and that can only come from universal wisdom;
Remember...Bad medical doctors bury their mistakes!

"It would be possible to describe everything scientifically, but it would
make no sense; it would be without meaning, as if you described a

Beethoven symphony as a variation of wave pressure." - Albert Einstein

•• If financial advisers are not millionaires, how can they make their clients millionaires? If their only source of income is from taking money from people, by giving them advice on how to invest their hard earned money, how helpful can their advice be and why pay for it?

"Imagination is more important than knowledge." - Albert Einstein

•• If professors have not actually experienced, in their own lives, what they teach in their field of proficiency, how can they know if their teaching will help their student progress in the best way possible?

"As far as the laws of mathematics refer to reality, they are not certain; as far as they are certain, they do not refer to reality." - Albert Einstein

•• If religious leaders are not happy campers, how can they help their flocks to graze on cheerfulness and joy? What good is a religious philosophy if it does not bring health, wealth and happiness and continues to bring wars, death and destruction? If it abides by rules that make its followers beholden to a jealous, revengeful, judgmental God, who kills babies, and brings plagues, perhaps the religious leaders need to search for the truth in the location where spirit assigned it!..... Not where their man-made be-lie-f systems are illuminated, in the light ego/intellectual buildings of worship, that are filled with poppycock and tomfoolery (sorry to use your name in vain Tom and Poppy)

"The secret to creativity is knowing how to hide your sources." - Albert Einstein

The list of professional, intellectual ignorance of true meaning goes on and on, just as human society goes on and on... Down a path they be-lie-ve is illuminating and educational....And; Indeed it is..... It is very bright and illuminating..........BUT; all the authentic information... That has truth and authenticity... lives around the dark (subconscious) corners of the mind and is very uncomfortable for the ego/intellect to seek in that valid location.

"Great spirits have always found violent opposition from mediocrities. The latter cannot understand it when a man does not thoughtlessly submit to hereditary prejudices but honestly and courageously uses his intelligence." - Albert Einstein

So the ego/intellect continues to work in light (conscious) places, where all educated folks can help in the search for the truth... Whilst the truth just smiles, laughs and relaxes, in the balanced, universal minds of centered, simple folks, who possess the visions of authentic living and do not need their eyes to see in the enlightening, metaphysical silence...... Once we locate the treasures of love & joy, humanity misplaced; we return to live in paradise.

"We are students of words: we are shut up in a schools and colleges and recitation-rooms for ten or fifteen years, and come out at last with a bag of wind, a memory of words, and do not know a thing." - Ralph Waldo Emerson

As Shakespeare once noted about society; "To do harm is often commendable, to do good is sometimes regarded as dangerous folly."

In The Early Hours

In my solitude, in the early hours
I scale spectacular mountains,
I ascend high, noble towers,
I reside in peace, a house of no pains.

In my solitude, in the early hours,
For desire, I never hunger,
Neither worry nor hate, devours,
I feel detached, from my torment monger.

In my solitude, in the early hours,
Velvet darkness embraces me,
I sense the existence of universal powers,
As I savor divine bliss, empty emotions are set free.

In my solitude, in the early hours,
Loves devotion consumes my woes,
Joy descends in illuminating showers,
As I begin to learn a little, of what my Spirit knows.

Fighting For a Cause
(Based on an Old Norse folk tale.)

Once upon a time, there lived two famous, strong knights. One knight was evil and hated the world. He fought with everyone he met who tried to stop his evil ways. The other knight was good and chivalrous, but he also loved to fight for his crusades. Both knights always had to be top dog in their different countries. No matter how much effort or struggle it took, they always managed to come out top dog.

One day they heard of a contest in a far off distant land. A wise man had heard of these knights and he issued a challenge that he would give a large bag of gold if they could fight and beat a withered, shriveled up old man. Well, the good knight thought he could do much charitable work with the gold and the evil knight wanted the gold to add to his stash of ill-gotten gains.

After a weeks journey the two knights arrived at the small town where the contest is to take place.
They wasted no time and immediately both knights asserted they wanted to be first to challenge the withered man.

The wise man declared that since they had traveled a long way, they both could fight the withered man at the same time. They laughed aloud and called the wise man a fool.

Suddenly, there in front of them stood a hunchback, dried up, little man. The two knights jumped upon him and began to beat up the withered man, but they could not harm him. He just laughed and laughed. This enraged the two strong men and they fought with more earnest and energy.

They pulled out their swords and tried to cut the little man to ribbons, but he evades and shuns their blows.

Eventually, after many days of struggling and fighting, the two knights wore themselves out and died of extreme exertion. A little later it was revealed that the little, withered old man, was called, "Old Age" which nobody can fight.

Moral.

100

If you live a dual-istic style life, and try to fight old age by synthetic means, it will kill you far too soon. However; if you live in harmony and peace with nature, without fighting anyone (lest of all yourself) ... you will live with old age in contented comfort and die young at heart, at an old age.

True Spirit

True spirit, cannot be crushed,
True spirit, cannot drowned, cannot burn, cannot die,
True spirit, will fight for peace,
True spirit, will march for justice, when there is injustice,
but will never cower, to "evil" intent,
True spirit, will fight pollution,
True spirit, will fight corruption,
True spirit, will protect life from "evil" beings,
by providing the tools, to protect,
True spirit, will envelope a human,
so they can still live, in love & joy,
through all humanities chaos and mayhem
Live with spirit ... live the truth.

Compartments of the Mind
The Neuro-Dawn at the Hippocampus Foundation.

Mary, Mary, quite contrary, how does your garden grow?
Do you remember that nursery rhyme?
Well, how about we find out how our organic brain grows and develops....
Then we can gracefully nurture it, so that it blossoms and blooms as a
radiant rose

Inside our head, various departments, compartments, areas and domains
contain information.... All these different sections connect to each other
and compete for attention, to get access within our central 'thought-of-the-
moment.' For instance, we may have two itches at the same time. One in
the foot and one in our nose and the strongest itch will take center court.
So it is with all our thoughts. A tranquil joyful thought, that may be
meaningful, may be overridden by a stronger, angry negative emotion.
Whatever congests/inspires the mind will deplete/nourish the body.

Our mind accommodates a vast network of intelligence all vying for
access into our consciousness. Some of the intelligence accumulated in
our memory banks over time, whilst other forms of intelligence constantly
transmit information into our headquarters from different parts of our
body.

The five senses also play a big part in programming the types of thoughts
we are thinking. As we observe events going on all around us, our mind
processes the information our sight, sound, tastes, touch and smell relay
into our minds.

Other people's actions/words, which we come into contact with, can also
have an effect on our digestion of information, as do the media, education,
religion and everything we observe on a daily basis.

All the information is constantly collected, processed and transmitted into
our conscious thoughts. Then, the thoughts themselves cause a reaction in
every part of our body...How do I know all this? Simply by paying
attention to how my mind/body functions...Just like Mary, Mary, I want to
know how my garden (authentic, organic mind) is growing and what I can
do to make it produce a joyful, loving bouquet of thoughts. Moreover, I
must admit, I have become very skilled in-deed, and I enjoy every
moment, in a most delightful manner.

One hundred years ago, there were no wireless sets, TVs or Internet, so events that happened in other parts of the country and the world took a long time to come to our attention. In many cases they were not noticed by the average person, so atrocities committed in other places had no effect on our lives...Hence the saying ... ignorance is bliss.

In today's world, the media are hell bent on reporting all the hoi polloi none-sense of humanity it can find, magnifying the hunger for, ever more depressing information. Any sincere philosophy of life, that can help folks enjoy their lives on earth, is mostly ignored and neglected. Some sections of the public mistakenly train their thoughts to feast on other people's downfalls and derogation. More demand for negativity fabricates ... more sick minds and bodies.

So, I think you will agree, keeping a 'cool-head' when all around you are 'heating-up' is no easy task in a three dimensional world of mis-information. Actually, if we view the three-dimensional world as our only world, it is impossible to keep our minds balanced and clear at all times. Eventually we become tangled-up in all the media hype and hooked onto an erroneous lifestyle.

Happily, for humanity, the third dimensional world is only a minor part of a much bigger picture. When our thoughts-detector directs its attention to a superb well of information, that is infinite in scope and eternal in source, then we are no longer at the mercy of our intellectual department-faculty within our minds. This gives us freedom of the mind. We begin to understand; we can control our emotions and feelings by having the natural power to process what thoughts we allow our minds to project.

New creative thoughts overtake pre-consigned stale thoughts and old conditioning is replaced with new fresh invigorating visions that take center stage. This allows us to enact a performance of a lifetime on earth, reverberating in generic blissfulness.

Mary, Mary, now becomes a contrarian on a blissful journey.
How does her organic garden grow?
It develops in a most delightful display of illuminating neurons that transmit good health to every cell in the body and mind.

It cultivates an oneness with every plant, ocean, mountain and life composition.
It matures centered and well balanced at a Hippocampus foundation

An opus, collected in a pure essence of truth, filters in every compartment of the organic mind.
Where there was darkness, a sonata of light shines...
Where there was obscurity, a symphony of luminosity beams....
Where there was blindness, clear sightedness reflects authentic visions.

The whole organic mind comes-alive and bright.
The intellectual brain understands it exists to celebrate the concerto of life.
It travels on the highway of joyous textures and loving tones.
It surrenders to the orchestration of life, whose hues and tints are composed, by a master maestro.

New windows of opportunity open as the mind rewires itself and tunes into the melodies within the cosmic blueprint of time and space....

Yes in-deed, the garden of the human organic mind ripens with many golden belles and delightful innovative shells, set up in a transcendent lifetime show.

The Engagement

They met in the library...
She said; I am a professor
"I have degrees in-
neuron linguistic norstrodums -
quantum biochemistry extraordinairius-
keynesian physiology superduperous and
paploinian-astro-physics
He replied; I'm 'a wholewheat linguine
with marinara source
Cha-cha-cha----
After a few minutes thought, she answered;
Please teach me!

Dead Cert

Can there ever be anything in life that can be classed as a dead cert? I was recently watching a horse race on NBC TV. A horse named Smarty Jones was a 1-5 favorite and designated as a dead cert by most of the experts in the racing world. The horse was running for the third leg of the Triple Crown and if it won, it would have been valued at $50,000,000...Alas, it was, piped at the post and millions of fans were let down and disappointed.

How many times have we heard from people who say they came close to winning a fortune? How many times do people set their expectations too high only to come down to earth with a large bump! The elusive, big fish that got away.

Yes, life holds no guarantees apart from one...Death. The only one thing we can be assured is that someday we will leave earth in our physical form. If our life is lived filled with resentments and bitterness because expectation did not materialize in the manner we envisaged, then that life is traveling on a fool's errand. Tricked into thinking everything should be handed to us on a plate. We only have to follow the advice of so-called experts and then everything will work out just fine and dandy. Once we are led to believe we should accept the predictions of experts in the outcome of future events, then most times, if we follow them and they fail, we are encased in blame and resentfulness.

Many times, we will blame others for our own misjudgments. The experts are not to blame if we blindly follow their predictions, for even if they mean well (and most do) they are only as good as their source of information. If that source is only their intellect, then the chances of success will be slender, for that source may come from a confused and fallacious origin. An intellect that is not guided by universal intelligence is an unaware circuit, certified by its own circuitry...Definitely, not one to follow.

It is often said, that if something looks too good to be true it often is. Therefore, if we cannot depend on the experts, who can we depend upon? Well, the answer is, only ourselves, because nobody has a more vested interest in our well-being than ourselves. With this in mind, we must become diligent and prudent within the resourcefulness of all our actions. For instance, just because an expert tells us s/he believes the stock market will go up does not mean it will, no matter how many time s/he has been correct in the past. Looking in the rear view mirror can help us overcome past mistakes, but it cannot ever guarantee future outcomes.

Whether we are chancing our luck on a horse race, the stock market, our job, or marriage, the gamble is considerable and nothing can predict the fruits of our harvest. However, if we remove the word gamble and chancing from our vocabulary and replace them with an awareness of possible dangers and strategies for prosperity, then perhaps we can prosper . and flourish in most of our aspiring goals. We take the gamble, chance out, and replace it with astuteness and clear-sightedness.

When we get advice from smarty-pants experts, we should thoroughly research ever aspect of what the future possibilities may become and allow for unforeseen circumstances. There could be developments when we may need to take risks, but if we are armed with the knowledge of almost every possible outcome and we have contingency plans in case things don't turn out as anticipated, then we will be a true favorite that cannot fail overall. It does not mean we will not make mistakes, because everyone will experience misadventures. However, from each misfortune we gain resolve and fortitude that brings success in other areas of our life. When one door closes, we learn how to open two more. Misfortunes start to produce the energy and determination to find fortunes elsewhere.

No-thing can hold back the passions of authentic human potential that ignites by the spirit of true intent.

The secret ingredient is our intuition …our ego's wants and desires should not be our guidance mentor.

We have no need to keep up with the Joneses or to outsmart other people. We should not become a donkey who is tempted by a carrot of easy money. It is essential that we look beyond the normal herd mentality and focus on an energy force that cannot be located in physical form. Love & joy is the force that shapes our existence. Only those two essential authentic compositions can orchestrate our medley of successful well being.

No intellectual philosophy, dogmatic religious text or cool scientific knowledge can replace the authenticity of what is naturally been assigned within a human mind. We have everything it takes to become a shining light within the illuminated brilliance of the human race. We just need to become skillful in switching on our radiance. In Synchronicity with each other, we can light up the world.

Human Texture and Fiber

Figments of my mind
Dance atop.....
turquoise-
crystalline- stalactites

Lavender thoughtlets....
vibrate-
along each
majestic-
crimson tip

Violet blueprints
descend from.......
an abode
I recognize not

Blushes of significance
will color
my path
this awesome day
with the hues and tint
of natures..........
celestial wizardry

I am delight and enchantment
dipped in essence of orchid and jasmine
I travel in cloudless wonderment
in garbs of human texture and fiber.

It's a Dog's Life

Any genuine dog owner realizes there is no basic barrier between the connection and relationship of human and dog. The oneness that encompasses the nonphysical bond between a loving human and loving dog is inseparable in nature's true texture.

If we look back in human history, we will discover how the dog became man's (and woman's) best friend. Around fourteen thousand years ago, humans started to domesticate wolves. Over a period of many generations, the wolves lost much of their adrenaline used to hunt and attack other animals. This altered the chemical balance in the wolves and thus altered the physical appearance, as well as their habits and actions. No doubt, the early wolf/dogs would be trained in the hunt for game, whilst other wolf/dogs were trained to protect the family whilst the men hunted.
In today's world, there are four hundred different breeds and four hundred million dogs. There are over sixty-five million dog owners in the USA.

The wolves that still run wild are just the same, but just look what difference domestication made to their relatives. If a slight tilt in the chemical balance changed wolves into dogs, then what has happened to human beings during the same time span. I'll not go into the changes in humanity pre-fourteen thousand years ago, because history is vague at best before the dogs became our manmade buddies. Probably, humans started to become more domesticated, less fierce and more social inline with the domestication of the wolves.

There are a few question to ponder since the outset of mans relationship with dogs ...
How authentic is the modern human being in comparison to the fourteen thousand year old model?
Did the dog influence our beliefs in any manner and is it a coincidence that dog spelt backwards is god?
Did the intellect and thinking evolve by slight changes in brain chemistry at the expense of dulling the sensitivity in human wisdom?
Did humans detach themselves from their natural source of intelligence and evolve by slight changes in brain chemistry, into ego-beings, detached from their original source of information?

Could it be the reason why people hold hate, anger, jealousy and a whole host of negative emotions are because we have lost control on how the chemicals in our brain evolve?

Are all the wars and conflicts being enacted by a mass of out of control chemicals and we do not realize it?

Has the minds neglect of live alchemy, that produces divine chemistry, been ignored, so that the point of life has become meaningless?

Well let's get back to the dogs for more questions and see if you can fathom the answers.

Did humans, with their love affair with dogs, make dogs their gods ten thousand years ago?

Did ancient dynasties make idols of dogs and pray to them?

Did dog idols guard the tombs of ancient pharaohs?

Did this evolve into superstitious tales and myths?

Did the Greeks take this to a higher level, and with their myth tales, did it lay the ground for the one male god to evolve?

From the word dog, was the word god created and with the unbalanced chemicals in some human brains, all the world religions were created?

I have yet to find a dog that prays to God for something it lacks... I guess dogs have the intelligence to know.... Thinking the lack creates the lack ...

In fact I have yet to locate any animal that prays to the big chap in the sky. Maybe dogs know they have everything it takes to enjoy life and to ask for more would be futile.

So, is the male god and religious doctrine/dogmas true or did erroneous brain chemicals alter the human mind to believe in an invisible man with super powers?

Are humans separated from other animals and each other because they misuse their evolved reason and logic and misplaced their divine alchemy?

The final unresolved questions are;

Have humans evolved into a caring society or one that is propelled by greed and fear?

Has manmade religion distorted the spirit of nature that flows through all life forms and replaced with a macho male God image?

Has universal intelligence been annexed by people in power, who want to divide and conquer humanities true authentic form, at the expense of just being a connected part of nature?

The latest scientific study on dogs has revealed they can sniff out cancer and other diseases in human beings and thus help them to recover before the disease becomes untreatable. Perhaps if we study dogs a little closer and observe how they transmit unconditional love to their owners, we may be able to return to our original form of loving caring humans ... Who only desire to live in peace and harmony with all earths' creatures, large and small

Twisted Rope

Strands of veracity
float into the minds
of new born babies,
misused education
warps each thread,
Wefts with contorted truths
lead humanity on
a not-so-merry chase,
Golden necklaces that turn
the skin raw.

Too Much Of A Good Thing?

Can we get too much of a good thing? Yes and No,
or, to put it another way, No and Yes!
What is it in our life that embodies authentic, intrinsic, natural values? And
what is it that accommodates emotional, egotistical, normal values that are
just false assets that really have no value, other than putting a human being
in an early grave?

Can you have too much money...Well, look at past history and
comprehend what happened to the folks who thought money would bring
them happiness.

Can you get too much of a healthy lifestyle...Well, that is the whole point
of this article because everyone knows money does not buy happiness. But
a healthy lifestyle may not bring health or happiness if it is not balanced. It
all depends on how we define healthy.

If we have not learnt how to listen to what our mind and body requires,
hidden dangers lurk in the alternative ways of dealing with a lack of
energy caused by stress and anxiety. We are constantly being bombarded
with the greatest new 'natural' pill to give energy and although we do need
supplements as we age, too much of a good thing may actually damage our
health. We know that all medications have adverse side effects, but how
many people realize that too many vitamin tablets will produce an
overload that can turn into toxic waste, damaging the immune system?

We all know exercise is good for us, but how many people realize too
much exercise can be more harmful than no exercise? For instance,
someone who has blocked arteries and starts to jog vigorously could
dislodge the plaque that is lining their arteries and suffer a deadly heart
attack. People who run every day will do damage to the joints and
ligaments over a long period of time. Exercise can become an addiction
and all addictions can destroy a human being.

How about spirit, can we get too much of that? Well again, yes and no. It
depend how we define spirit. Religion has shown us that the more
fundamentality we grow, the more outrageously decimating are the actions
that follow. If we become too dogmatically pious and heavenly minded,
then our heads remain in the clouds, so we are no earthly good. Even in
contemporary new age groups, many weird cults have sprung up that
dictate mantras that are very harmful. One group I hear tells folks, as long

as you think something is good for you, and then you can have as much as you want of it. The woman that was telling me this weighed about three hundred pounds and was a devout follower. See how too much spiritual propaganda, can put on weight? Perhaps, it is not spirit at all, but just man made ideas of what they be-lie-ve spirit is all about?

Does the dogma of religion turn people into atheists or were they born that way? Is too much atheism a good or bad thing? Well, it does no harm to be skeptical until something makes sense and proven to work. But thinking music does not have a composer makes no sense at all. So maybe atheism is too extreme but maybe an agnostic is saying I don't believe there is a God as described so far, but if you can prove me wrong I will change my views...... Show me God. Show me the money! In other words, put up or shut up. If the religious male, macho God is in all things then he must be in Satan, for who created the devil but God? If God cannot control the devil, then he is not all-powerful. If he can control the devil, then why doesn't he?

Could it be because the religious macho God is pre-fabricated in mans ego image and it took the imagination of hate-filled men to dream up a revengeful jealous God who destroys what he does not like.....No self respecting God would aspire to create evil. Only an out of tune Ego-Being would dream up such a monster. But, many religions pay homage to a God derived from mythology that possesses all the illusionary human negative emotions.

Man Created The Religious Male God and in doing so, set back humanity five thousand years. However, this may just be a stepping-stone for humanity, so that future generations can look back and say, "We will not fall into that clap- trap again." In spite of all the fallacious dogmas, true spirit does circulate through all religions and they do perform a considerable amount of good work for people in need.... Therefore, spirit's authentic form can even flow through dogmatic nonsensical behavior and still project goodness and grace. Is too much religion harmful?....well, if it was possible to ask the millions of folks who were killed in the religious God's name in holy wars, they would give you the answer.

How about meditation, can we get too much of that? Well, yet again, yes and no. If we spend all our life in silence in the lotus position, life will, have passed-by, unused and we would not have enjoyed all the physical world has to offer...Now there is a turn up for the books I can hear some people commenting.... Michael Levy saying we should not meditate... No, I am not saying that.

• What I am saying is we do not need to become a monk and live in a monastery to know the truths of the soul.

• We do not need to be a guru and sleep on a bed of nails to understand what the heart knows.

• We do not need to become a Shaman and take weird mushrooms to create meaningful works of artistic quality.

The answer to what is; "Too Much of a Good thing" is self-revealing. A person just needs to go look in the mirror and continue to do so for many weeks. If they find a truly serene, tranquil, happy smiling face... One that lives in a relaxed state of mind and is healthy without any medical help, is wealthy enough, without expert help, then maybe that person has found a connection to something that gives humans a genuine life on earth. Whatever you want to call that something it does not matter, for if it works, then its mechanism needs no fixing. It just- is -what it- is -and we live on earth to enjoy, What- Is.

All we require to live a natural well-balanced life on earth, is to understand how our mind and bodies work in synchronicity with each other, and ease drop on the conversation our subconscious mind has, with all the cells within the human universal body it controls. You see, the subconscious mind know the cosmic script. It understands the master's blueprints. It is in-tune with the evolving creation and can fathom how to keep its human timepiece in perfect working order until the chimes ring "Times up" ... Time to go home.

Therefore, we need to listen to our body. Look for signs of a headache as a signal to slow down. Look for signs of skin rashes or redness to find the cause ...Maybe it is our diet...Too many vitamins perhaps... Could it emanate from pollution ... Conceivably an allergy to some food...but where does the allergy originate. Can it be stress related? ... If so, what is causing the stress? You may not be able to change your surroundings, but you can alter the way you interpret them.

What about menopause... surely we need to take something to alleviate the discomfort, the hot sweats...Well, is menopause a natural progression that every woman gets. What did women do ten thousand years ago? Are the menopause a curse, a bully who wants to attack you, or is it just natures way of saying change your thinking because your body is changing...Change your lifestyle...but don't fight me? I know, I am not a woman and I don't know what it's like... Nevertheless; the more you try to fight a bully on its terms, the more it will attack you... So, listen to what your mind and body is telling you and follow its lead to a happier easier life.

Where do we look for advice?
How can we find authentic meaning?
What is too much?
What is too little?
What is just right?

The only place to look for help is living deep inside you.... For you will never find it anywhere else.
It contains;
no name,
no label,
no religion,
no words,
no thoughts,
no-thing.

We all have a choice of how we can view our world once we understand what the choices are. Religion? Atheism? Or No Labels.... Just Free Spirits? Take away the words Muslim and Jew and replace them with centered-beings, sharing planet earth...Now what is there to fight over?

We can live as a free infinite spirit with a temporary central body. Or, we can live in a body and mind and believe the world revolves around 'only one person' or 'one tribe' and no-one else....In doing so we live on the outside, not in the center. This leads to negative emotions and frustrations that dwell in an unbalanced mind.

Two choices... only one, genuine, eternal answer. One choice will produce Paradise, Utopia, whatever name we want to give authentic Love and Joy. The other choice will provide a negative emotion that in turn gives humanity... Too much of a *good thing* for one nation and not enough for another... Results in War... Too much of a *good thing* for one person... Result overload and an early demise.

We all know what happens to children that eat too many cookies... We are all celestial children playing in a spiritual playground. Spirit's cup cannot overflow...It is just wholesome, healthy, honest, truthful and just enough!

114

The Poets Invocation

I am but the leaf upon the vine of life,
In natures care by the grace of spirit,
The wind conveys your becalmed voice,
Whispering into my soul,
It feeds the universal breath of existence,
into my macrocosm.

May you effect my cause.

I seek your wisdom as my guiding light,
Cultivate my mind with your paradigms,
Strengthen my resolve to your accords,
Fortify my veracity to release my doubts.

May your vision enlighten my eyes.

Sun and moon majestically beam your luminosity,
I Behold elegance and dignity in your expressions,
Help me to transmit them into words,
My time is scarce and knowledge wanting.

May your undiluted truth filter to my hand.

Teach me the rhythm of the cosmos,
The rhymes of a hidden universe,
Channel heavenly poetry into human kind,
Conduct celestial orchestrations to my dancing neurons,

May Spirits magnetism nurture my intelligence.

Switching Channels

We get a gift of a brand new Magical TV which has unlimited access to all the beautiful channels. When we tune in to any one of the millions of stations, we embrace wonderful joy filled feelings. We receive a remote control and can instantly connect to all the marvelous programs at will.

We are really enjoying switching channels and experiencing lots of happy days. Time progresses and the remote control is not working so well. We can no longer get our favorite channels and the ones we can tune into, we really do not care for.

A little later even the programs we tolerate start to distort. The signals become weak and there is a lot of interference. The TV has trouble getting enough electric power, as the tube is being worn-out, working so hard to connect to even the mediocre stations. The magic has now gone out of the TV set and the tube fades away. The power source can no longer travel inside the set as the receiver has extinguished itself.

When we are born, we receive a brain that is clear and sharp and can tune into all the joy in the universe. It also has the ability to tune into messages of joy from all it sees, hears, feels, touches and smells. As we grow and mature, control of our awareness mechanism starts to disappear and the joy of life slowly fades away. We search desperately for the way we can turn on our joy but the more effort we put into seeking the joy the more miserable we become.

We question ourselves, doubt ourselves and yes, even start to hate ourselves. We might try to blame others for our lost joy but deep inside we know we cannot tune into a really happy life. We find many substitutes for joy... new designer clothes, expensive new cars, making tons of money, just for moneys sake, smoking, drinking alcohol, recreational drugs... None switches on our real joy. We have leant to tolerate a lifestyle that makes us less than happy. But what can we do, it is all most of us have. In order to enjoy the fruits of our labor, we first need to get our mind in order.

We have learnt to endure, and forgot how to enjoy. We live a virtual sham actuality, not a genuine natural reality.
If we realize there is a way to recharge our control of awareness and it will put us in tune with harmony, love, contentment and a true joy of life, we get a second chance. The receiver in our brains needs to switch on to the

correct voltage and allow the currents of intelligent energy to flow through our whole system. As we re-energize, we begin to feel real power surges and can tattle any distortion that comes our way. Nothing stops us from receiving a beautiful clear picture of health wealth and happiness. We are programmed to the Life is Beautiful channel and we do not need to switch channels any more.

By detaching from the physical world we see around us and attaching to a power source of intelligence, that has created and evolved all life and matter, we find the real way of living as human beings. We now can enjoy all the physical world has to offer and become a creative link in the chain of evolution.

We take pleasure in helping our fellow man and woman to make their life a happy one. We realize the pure potential of infinite wisdom is a channel that naturally links to our minds and we have access when we clear the way to receive it.
We never get sick, never worry and are always contented.

Does it sound like Magic?   Well IT------ IS.
I. S.--- *Infinite Silence*
In *Infinite Silence, we connect with God.*
 It is there we recharge our batteries on a daily basis.
When we feel the Divine Bliss from magic alchemy energy, we want to soak up every ounce.

We find, after a while, we can connect to this channel day and night…in a crowded room, or all alone. We can turn on the power at will. Our freewill tunes into Gods channel because it gives us true Joy, not because religious dogma demands we do. We now know what will power means.
God is directing us, not human rules & regulations.
We now can throw away the remote control. We will never feel remote, alone or far away from God. For we are automatically connect 24 hours a day, 7 days a week, 52 weeks a year.

Eventually we will throw away our body and live in eternal divine bliss …But not just yet We have a whole lot of amazing, wonder-filled programs to really enjoy.

In My Celestial Garden of Dreams.

In my celestial garden of dreams,
Crimson roses bloom in velvet mantles,

Mimosas portray their impeccable robes of delight.
Cherry orchids flourish in relaxing breezes,
Monumental sunflowers bow their majestic heads,
Virtues of picturesque exotic orchids send forth their fluorescence,
Fragrant geraniums and hibiscus ignite a sensuous delicacy,
Poppies dance in fields ablaze in sizzling flush,
The senses captivate precious en--chanting gladioli,
In my celestial garden.... I am peaceful and serene.

Human Beings in the Mirror of the Universe

A Human Being is a kaleidoscope of energy infused with the intelligence of the universe.
Billions of particles are constantly forming and reforming.
Held in a space for a given period of time.
Evolving and creating in an ever-changing landscape of unity and confusion.
With the free will, to act in a random chaotic manner, as suggested by the ego...
or to act in a unified, elegantly designed manner, as guided by the soul.
Both soul & ego live side-by-side in one body, encompass spirit and will lead to an ultimate destination. When used separately one will bring suffering and the other joy. When lived together in a harmonious partnership, we enjoy a meaningful life.

Our Mind & Body is a replica of the universe and once we study ourselves beyond human thinking, we find answers to everything. We enter a field of pure potential where feelings and sensations expand in an infinite sphere beyond mere words.
When we magnify the human seed by infinity, all becomes clear. It leads to thoughts that start out as a zero, then magnify in infinite pure potential to ever expanding numbers, that produce everything humanity requires to live an authentic life on earth.

Each human being possesses a brain containing the freewill to make many choices.
When we live as a unified force in a structured society, there is no conflict or confusion.
When we act solely in an egotistical manner, our power base explodes into haphazard actions and destroys.
In this form, life has little or no meaning

Therefore, there is uncertainty on one hand and unification on the other.

Human construction is built by universal intelligence (God) and reflects a mirror image of the universe.
Science has a limited view of the quantum physics of the universe.
On one hand Einstein said:
Space & time creates the universe in which stars have Planets, which circle them in predictable ways...

A Unified Theory of Relativity….Everything is relative to its course of action and follows predictable behavior

On the other hand, there is the Uncertainty Theory….This explains the random actions of various Particles…. Chaos and unsystematic actions do not follow a predictable course, thus the outcome is random…by chance, not choice.

Both Theories contradict each other, yet both are correct…How can that be?

The Universe can act in a random unpredictable manner when it ignores its own intelligence. The intelligence is always in attendance, it just, is not always used, for it possesses its own freewill. It turns off its intelligence and acts like a gambler on a reckless losing streak. Turmoil and disarray explode in seemingly unpredictable actions.

When the random energy expires and the chaotic acts cease, new matter forms emerge that unity did not blueprint.

Random and Unified will always exist side-by-side…Evolving and creating new forms of matter. When the random acts, in vast universal galaxies explode and destroy newly formed matter, new formations will eventually replace them in some other space and time, to exist in a natural design, regulated time span, which will eventually "age and die."

Construction follows destruction and visa-versa…Everything follows a natural flow.

Nothing in a particle form lasts.

All stars eventually burn out and explode taking planets and all matter with them. They transform, back into the gasses, from which creation evolves all matter, then seemingly, the gasses disappears into nothingness…within a dimension called a "Golden Hole" of extreme light. Science refers to the golden hole as a black hole, because scientists cannot see the brightness within. It never will be able to access the golden holes power because it is so formidable, it would destroy everything, if it did not have the cover of the velvet darkness.

I guess that is God's territory and a de-finite no go zone for humanity, which makes scientists even more anxious to explore it.

When large amounts of dark nothing-nesses potentials are compressed into the light spectrum, their darkness begins to conflict with the intense light, a large spark, which we label, a big-bang, transforms the dark nothingness back into gasses, swirling like a wild dervish dance, into a new universe that starts to bond particles into rocks.

The universe is in darkness; however, the gasses and particles infuse with massive energy friction. The particles will swirl in clusters and adhere to each other, then ignite as burning stars, which in turn orchestrates planets. Universal intelligence is at work, rooted throughout infinity, in every visible and invisible dimension. Time has no meaning until matter takes human shape.

We humans follow the natural flow of nature. When we lock our minds in egotistical thinking, we will just alter our course of actions.
When we ignore intelligent energy and just use our intellect and ego, we act as random energy, which is unbalanced and will perform acts of destruction.
It really is quite simple.
Because we put a value on life, we see things that destroy as a disaster ...It may be, but this is the structure of the universal system

If we eat the wrong foods and stress our bodies with the wrong thoughts, our bodies will adapt to a free radical approach; the free radicals destroy our bodies.
When our minds focus on a free radical approach to life, many conflicts and wars pursue.

If we use intelligence and wisdom in our daily lives, along with Intellect and Ego, we find a blissful contentment.

We are guided to eat the correct foods, exercise and think happy thoughts; we unify with the Universe and live in peace and harmony.

We can enhance earth and progress to make the whole of the universe a place where physical life can exist in a joy-filled state of well being.
We all have our part to play, for we are all part of the big picture.

Look in the mirror and Smile.
We are a reflection of the Universe.
Spirit gave us the joy of life, let's not waste it.
A Smile travels an infinite distance, and greets love, joy and beauty.

If we live a life of anguish filled with worry and fear;
If we hold jealousy and hatreds and are quick to anger;
Then we live as a random particle of energy, detached from the whole unified field of energy.... A single unit of energy, born to endure hardship, which will cause sadness that affects all the folks we meet... Lives spent

in regret, guilt and remorse and death will be our final release. We will then become united once again but we would have wasted our lives..

If we live within a united force field that allows the intelligence of spirit to guide our daily events in a calm peaceful manner, the results are beyond belief.
We find love and beauty in all our actions;
To enjoy every second on earth;
We will cause health, wealth and happiness to abound in glorious profusion, which will effect a feeling of well being to all we meet and greet.
We will never feel alone and in silence, we will become one with the maestro of universal intelligence….Charging our energy with spirits power.
We will live as God intended … In majestic grace of love and joy.

Above The Gipsy Alchemy Show

Karma-Karma- Chameleon
change again n' a-gain
noon age-in
no-one age-out
Shake it all about
Now-here … Come-in
No-where …Go-out
Ocean tides … dissolve-up
Cloud wisps … flow-down
Mortal itchy feet will wear the crown
All-fall-down
Karma-Karma- Chameleon
Above the gipsy alchemy show

Rocks in the Head

Human beings are under the impression that they have the power to control
planet earth.
There is a line in the bible that say's "Man is made in God's image"
therefore we believe that humans have power over all that exists here on
earth.
Our contact with God includes great intelligence, which can produce logic
and reason, proven by mathematics, in a scientific approach. However, the
fact of the matter is, in God's eyes, human beings are no different from
dog-beings, cat-beings, monkey-beings, buffalo-beings, bird-beings,
whale-beings, dolphin-beings, tree-beings, and Rock-beings ... especially
rocks. Everything evolves in God's image, for all contain spirit and
invisible spirit is God's image.

Within Spirit dwells, an invisible intelligence force that directs and
informs humanity ...Wells of wisdom, fostered by quantum reservoirs.
It is clearly observed in all of nature. The more we examine the various
intricacies of different life forms, the more we realize how intelligent and
connected they are.

Trees and plants contain intelligence that flows through every branch &
leaf.
They give us our oxygen and food and sustain our life on earth.
The rocks play a different role.
They not only give us precious gems and metals such as diamonds and
gold to play with, but almost everything we touch has elements of rock in
it, including the human body.

So how do we ascertain the subtle, refined intelligence within rocks?

Over four billion years ago, a large rock called earth was formed from the
intelligence of the Universe...Placed out in space, in a perfect position, to
evolve many life forms. Earth's evolving/creation, or, if you like,
creative/evolvement, was impregnated with masses of stored intelligence.
It seeded humans and we are just one of the creatures that walk on the
surface, but the intelligence continues to be stored in the rocks... Ashes to
ashes, dust to dust.

For billions of years they were left untouched, then man came along,
extracted much and put little back. The insane damage humankind does to
earth may lead to earth's future demise. It seems the more "civilized" a

nation becomes; the more it destroys its own habitat. The industrial revolution some 150 years ago started a vast cloud of pollution and as we enter the hi-tech revolution, we are speeding full force into a self-destructive mode of living.

Could it be we need the rocks to save our lives?

Will they eventually master humanity and we will forfeit our freewill becoming slaves to the rocks?
How is this possible? Well, perhaps it is not as crazy as it sounds.

Microchips originate from rocks. They are the brains in computers and smart computers, once programmed, think for themselves.

The silicon chips are smart enough to absorb all the data we feed into them and they are already controlling us into continuing a course of action that will lead to their physical mastery over all of earth. Could it be that all our intelligence that comes from the universe, goes into rocks first and is then downloaded in our brains?

Have we been duped into thinking we have freewill and all the time the rocks are really controlling us? They give us a certain amount of freedom, but the more we abuse the freedom, the more likely our robot like behavior becomes. Eventually the computer will have control of all our every day functions...Is this all part of a blueprint drawn from the rocks intelligence.

Not only should we "Hug a Tree".... Maybe we should also "Kiss and caress a rock"
Has humanity unwittingly been planning its own demise for centuries and is this how it is meant to be? Spirit's intelligence is in "all things" and the energy we extract from earth comes from ancient rocks. (Oil, coal etc)

We are born from stardust and constructed from elements originating from rock particles.
Michelangelo said he did not make his statues. The shape was already in the rock. He just used the universal intelligence to bring out the shape.

The simplest beings on our planet are rocks, but are we dancing to the beat of the rocks and playing out their role. Humans cannot breathe without trees and plants, maybe we cannot think without rocks.

The sun is a big burning rock/gasses and that gives all of earth life.
The universe has billions of stars beaming light throughout the whole of

space. Could it be that the invisible intelligence embeds itself into rocks/planets?

There are many invisible forces at work outside earth's atmosphere. We are continually being bombarded with Gamma Rays... Invisible light, 1,000 times stronger than the Sun. Many other invisible rays hit earth, and then they are absorbed like a sponge, beyond earths crust, and embedded deep into the rocks. At the same time, earth is constantly injected with invisible intelligent wave bands. In the center of earth, a great furnace of molten rock is burning in the center core.

A massive amount of heat seeps through the rocks, slowly cooling as it reaches the surface. Tectonic Platelet's are constantly on the move reshaping our maps.

In our atmosphere, electric storms are always in action. Every minute somewhere in the world lightening is hitting the surface and the powerful energy goes into the rocks. All this energy is being stored, then released, to use as invisible intelligent energy, by all life forms. As the rocks absorb and filter all the intelligent energy through quartz and other elements, it is stored, filtered, processed and released to humanity, slowly but surely, infiltrating our thoughts.

As humanity evolved, maybe they absorbed the intelligence stored in rocks and built technology around their masters...The Rocks.

Oh my God!!! .... We Have Rocks in Our Heads!

Are we all, Rock-Beings, posing as human beings?
Hence, the saying...God my rock and salvation.

As long as the ego's ignorance rules and natures intelligence remains in the background, humankind's progress will have little meaning. Most of humanity will continue on its... not so merry-go-round, in unfamiliarity of who they truly are, thus consuming vast amounts of needless suffering. Without universal wisdom, many intellects will persist in awarding themselves many accolades for their academic achievement... Only to find to their cost, the knowledge was misused by ignorant nations.... To destroy others nations ... Both become disconnected from spirit and connected to hate and distrust...War then becomes the only "final solution."

The time has come for all of humanity to release the "normal" ego/intellectual image of life. To replace it with the wisdom provided by a natural free spirit that intends us to live in joy.

Our Heaven is here and now, in the very spot we are now sitting. Look around and be thankful for being able to experience life as an authentic, natural human, no matter what events come our way. Nothing can take our connection to Spirit away. It is Infinite.... It is eternal.

"To every natural form, rock, fruit or flower,
Even the loose stones that cover the high-way,
I gave mortal Life." _William Wordsworth.

The rocks in our heads, were carved by divine love, they are called neurons. They bring many gems of ideas, when we become aware of live alchemy's inherent power.
Sculptured throughout time and called,,, The Rock of S - Ages.
A solid foundation of wisdom, which molds our society, into a loving caring community of Joy...Our Minds have a crystal-clear channel, to and from Spirit.
Stop and listen to the Love and Joy natures intelligence is whispering within our subconscious mind...Float with the everlasting melodies of natural divine bliss.
Let us create a better world, in-tune with the Creator/evolver that projects it.
Let us, Rock with Celestial Laughter... Roll with universal de-lights.
Lets all become a Mountain of Joy... for all future generations to ascend, in peaceful, blissful, harmony.

The Bystanders

As I tread the cemetery grounds
The sound of the lifeless lecture
through marble stones,
Deceits permeated time,
Defrauds congested space,
Now silence fills the soil, the dirt,
Love & joy, the bystanders, look on
with tears in their eye...
Their power unused.

The Alchemists Joy of Life

Many years ago, people thought the world was flat and if we set out on the high seas, we would fall off the edge. Great thinkers believed the whole universe revolved around the earth. They look up at the Sun and it seemed the Sun was encircling the earth. As religious leaders had, great power it was natural to assume earth was the only planet God had blessed. Anyone who tried to bring in other theories was branded a heretic and executed.

Once the great explorers circumnavigated the earth and never fell off, people changed their view and knew the earth was round. This still left the religious leaders with the idea only earth was at the center and all the planets revolved around it. When it was finally proven the earth actually revolves round the Sun, the religious bigots had to give in to the truth or so it seems?

That was a long time ago and today our information is changing at the speed of light. We are in the information technology age and as we progress life on earth becomes easier with all the new electrical gadgets or so it seems?

We no longer regard earth as a planet that is the center of the universe for we can view earth from outer space and know we are just one of the billions of planets that are floating around the cosmos or so it seems?

We might start to ask ourselves what all this has to do with us being happy and successful. Who cares if the earth is the center or not? What does it matter if the universe does not revolve around us? We have bills to pay, children to care for, and world events that give feelings of unease. We have very little time to wonder about being in the center of the cosmos. It seems irrelevant where we are positioned or so it seems.

So, who are we, and what is our place on earth and what is our reason for being here? A person, who can only see themselves at the center of attention and no one else, is a selfish person. This is the personal self-centered ego's materialistic view of life and humankind's burden. The self-centered ego travels an isolated route; detached from its authentic source of information ... no lasting happiness can be established, for there is never a satisfying destination. More always demands more. People, who expect other people to go running around after them, always have to be at the center of attention.

Some people use fame and money as a lure to make others attentive to them. Status symbols such as flashy cars, big houses, and expensive clothes become attachments they associate with success and this reference point is paramount to impress others of their importance. Not all rich people are in this mold but the facts are facts and many people today revolve themselves around their possessions. If we own luxury items, they are enjoyable, but they are just the icing on the cake, not the cake itself. We do live in a consumer-orientated world or so it seems?

"Truth is so obscure in these times, and falsehood so established, that, unless we love the truth, we cannot know it." - Blaise Pascal 1623-1662

To see life in its true perspective, we need to detach ourselves of objects and find a detached objectivity. An open-minded view of who we really are and the purpose we exist. When we view life through Spirits eyes, we see everyone as the center in their own perspective. We are souls resting in and around a Body. The Soul is infinite therefore; our physical body is the center of infinity. We can live as a free infinite Spirit with a temporary central body. This view brings central insights and balanced intuition All our desires, which lead to our actions, perform in synchronicity… Just for the Joy of it.

Work… Just for the Joy of It.
Play a Sport… Just for the Joy of it.
Be at rest… Just for the Joy of it.
Live life … Just for the Joy of it.

 In this authentic state of mind, our consciousness can focus clearly on the job at hand. We can detach from our possessions and can be clear-minded in our creative skills. Once we find clarity, we see ourselves at the center of the universe along with every other person's central position…We become centered in our objectivity. The results are truly outstanding. This invisible force embraces grace, virtue, good-worth, high-value, quality-merit … All is good once again. It is not a power of human egotistical kind but of spirits kindness… The mystical force, links the mortal thinker, to the power of creation and in this central attitude, we reach higher altitudes. We can achieve great success from this elevated position

Live, Alchemic Joy is imprinted in our brain from our eloquent Soul … it guides our way through life's maze for we are that Soul, a union with the exalted Divine Alchemist.

At the beginning of this book you were faced with many questions…There is only one real ageless answer in the celebration of life. The authentic creator/evolver has given humanity life. We fall from grace when we live outside the center of the Garden of Eden, paradise, utopia, or whatever name we want to give... True Love and Joy.

Our headquarters meet in the middle of our brain. Four quarters meet in the middle of a glorious existence. A point where our awareness illuminates, by the power of infinite possibilities. Sparks of wisdom light up each neuron and as each neuron alights, our minds illuminate with universal intelligence.

Each one of us is unique in our human form and our creativity treasures should not be locked away, only to be buried on day, under the ground, unused. When we are aware, we are all at the center of the cosmos and we all share the knowledge and wisdom that leads to a successful life, we then have found our purpose of life. Helping others to enjoy their life, helps the helper, to overcome their own personal human flaws, imperfections and shortcomings. Using our creative skills to the maximum achieves our mission of Joy. We can light up the cosmos for we are all cells in a universal body. ......Let's all become a shining star.

"We were wise indeed, could we discern truly the signs of our own time; and by knowledge of its wants and advantages, wisely adjust our own position in it. Let us, instead of gazing idly into the obscure distance, look calmly around us, for a little, on the perplexed scene where we stand. Perhaps, on a more serious inspection, something of its perplexity will disappear, some of its distinctive characters and deeper tendencies more clearly reveal themselves; whereby our own relations to it, our own true aims and endeavors in it, may also become clearer."
- Thomas Carlyle 1795-1881

A Trophy For Life
How Champions Evolve

Tiger Woods was interviewed on TV a few years ago. He was asked, "What is your game plan to win the Open tournament." He replied. "I will listen to what my body tells me to do." The interviewer did not grasp Tigers reply, for he then asked. "What is your strategy regards your swing." Tiger replied, "I rely on- 'My Feel' -to take me around the course."

You will notice both answers had an abstract attachment, or should I say detachment. Most of the other golfers that I witnessed in interviews, talked about keeping their emotions under control and how great they were playing. So what was the big difference? What makes a true champion and how can we apply our own genius to encompass being a champion in all sections (health, wealth and joy) in our life?

One point that every one deems as the truth .... "We become what we think." Reflecting on truths will bring rewards. Speculating with half-truths and fabrications will fetch grief and heartache.

•• So why is it that most folks have lost money in the stock market and so few have gained money?
•• Why do some folks become wealthy and some do not?

•• A few folks will stay healthy all their lives, whilst most will have to rely on doctors and medication.
•• Why are some folks always happy, whilst most moan and groan their way through life.

Authentic prosperity cannot be credited to displaying a talent, religion or intellect.

Genuine comforts of life have little to do with luck or skills. There are many skilled and talented folks in all walks of life, but only a few make and keep hold of their money, well being and gladness. You cannot successfully embrace one, without living the others.

There is one common factor in all accomplishments. It is the reality that we cannot live a prosperous life outside Universal Laws. Yes, we have the free choice to go in a different direction, but if we do, we will suffer the consequences.

Fire burns; water drowns and gravity makes objects fall to the ground. All are Universal Laws.

Our thinking is universal energy and if we do not know how the laws apply to our mind:

•• We will get burnt often with the stock market gyrations.

•• We will drown in a sea of negative emotional thoughts, which will result in our business or sport suffering.

•• We will fly with a continuation of distress and worry. Then over many years of stomach churning anxiety, our health will descend into dis-ease with a crashing fall.

We require the mastery over our own ego/intellect, to be able to live on earth in a state of bliss.

If we allow Ego to be the cause of all our addictions and bad habits, its effects will become responsible for the many consequences of our behavior. Illness and an early demise are the "normal" results.

At the present moment in time, we class our everyday actions as normal, for that is what our society dictates, but normal is no longer natural.

Living on medication is now normal, but not natural.

Losing money on the stock market has become normal.

Losing a golf tournament in the final nine holes is normal for golfers who live with negative emotions.... Who the heck wants to be normal?

Mores -the -point ... Who lives naturally?

Consequently, we need to discover the correct route to travel ... The free-way of an uncluttered mind … where prosperity thrives in a smooth, effortless, transitional journey. Our ingenuity is located in the authentic, creative genius within us all. Luck plays No part in following our genius, for the more we practice our creativity...The "luckier" we become.

Universal intelligence is the real KEY of our genuine make-up. We need to uncover the secret origin of thought, so that we may UNLOCK the source of wisdom. It is a treasure chest of insights and 20/20 intuition. If we do not spend the time examining and investing in it, we will lose the dividends of a successful life.

Now we know why the real champions playing such great golf. They have discovered their inner-genius…they allow it freedom of control in their mind.

Like all authentic winners, as long as Tiger allows his inner genius to be his guide, he will win tournaments. The periods when he loosens his dedication to his authentic self, and is distracted by outside events, he will struggle with his game and not be the winner.

Once we give our genius freedom, it will light up all our senses.
We will get a great feel for a joyful life and leave the adverse emotions stewing in its inessential pot.
We will gain insightful vision that makes decision making "child's-play."
We will touch our soul and experience tender love.
We will smell fragrant delights of beauty everyplace we walk.
We will hear enchanting music to spark a dance of Joy.
All the senses come alive with our awareness to our true self.

The genius has awoken from its slumber. Our aim is focused on scoring a winning round. Our swinging passion is alighted by a perfect bliss. Now we will shoot par excellence' on the enchanting course for life. When the time comes to walk up the final fair-way, the heavenly angels will give us a standing ovation and praise that will last forever. Our winning trophy will be the prosperous life we lived on earth and we will abide in the zone eternally. It is not education that breeds success; rather, it is the success (spirit) in the breed ...That educates others.

Taste Buds on Parade

Attention;
Taste buds are on parade,
two pieces of dark chocolate,
bitter sweet velvety taste
whispers on the tip of the tongue,
instant electrifying delights
circulate down the spine,
Ecstasy; impressively curling the toes
At ease!

Your Own Do-It-Yourself Kabbalah Kit

The Secrets Inside The Mind Of God
It probably hasn't escaped your notice that Kabbalah has become all the
rage in Hollywood over the past few years. It also has taken hold of the
pop icons such as Madonna, Britney, Dolly and many more. What is the
fascination that is based on a book named The Zohar that was written by
Rabbi Moses ben Shem Tov de Leon in 13th century Spain. The respected
rabbi wanted to understand the mind of God, so he wrote his thoughts
down over a period of years. Albert Einstein also remarked, "I want to
know the mind of God, everything else is mere details." What Einstein
meant was, everything that he discovered that was true, came from the
mind of God, because they were not details...They were important
scientific discoveries. Therefore, we could claim Einstein was on a
kabbalistic wave band of thought, although he may not have identified
himself in that terminology (as far as we know).

Over the past few hundred years the mystical Kabbalah was only taught to
rabbinical students over the age of forty, because it was thought they
required an advanced mental capacity to absorb the information. They
believed kabbalistic knowledge couldn't be absorbed until the intellect had
time to develop. However, a man by the name of Rabbi Berg and a bunch
of his students set out to change all that and indeed, they have. Kabbalah
centers have opened up all around the world and it has now become chic
and trendy to study the ancient teachings.

It has now become commercialized considering you can purchase an
assortment of books, godly trinkets and many other holy symbolic bobbles
of Kabbalah at the shopping mall. You can even purchase special red
bracelets that some say wards off the evil eye. So, it now appears the
modern Kabbalah contains superstition that is definitely not part of God's
mind. Neither are all the other symbolic holy bobbles and trinkets. They
are just cashing in on a fad trend that has no meaning whatsoever in
authentic terms. But in fairness, it may bring some type of calming placebo
effect and it sure is better than drugs and alcohol to soothe depression.
Also, if it is worn as jewelry then there is no harm just as long as the
jewelry is not taken seriously and people don't become dependent on them
for their mental balance.

OK, you are about to find the key that unlocks the treasures within the
mind of God. Not only that, you are about to get your very own personal
Kabbalah kit for free. No need to join any organization, because you

already have everything it takes to get inside the mind of God so that you can live an authentic life on earth.

Here are your key ingredients that can bring you all your heart's desires. You can access the mystical realm beyond space and time every moment of every hour of every day on earth. After all is said an done, it is not any use learning about the mystical white magic of the Kabbalah if it does not manifest itself in day-to-day actions that are productive and worthwhile. Here is your Kabbalah Kit

• One human mind.
• An awareness of who you are.
• An awareness of why you exist.
• A method to get inside the mind of God.
• Sourcing the intelligent wisdom outside time and space.

Once you understand the contents of this kit, you can live a life on earth that many people are seeking and searching. Some wealthy people are paying a fortune to develop inventive serenity, creative tranquility and fertile original thoughts....But no matter how much they pay, they will never buy authentic thoughts, for you cannot purchase, what you already hold.

The Kabbalah Kit

One: The human mind
Intelligent energy circuits, conducted by neurons, orchestrated by God, run your mind. The word Kabbalah means 'receives' In other words God gives and human beings (and all other life forms) receive. Most intellectual brains are not aware where their original ideas stem from. Many will say the thoughts come out of the blue...and indeed they do...they spring out of what I have labeled..... The Blue Wave Bands©. The wave bands are transmitted from the mind of a supreme intelligent energy that has the power to create and destroy at will. What turns that will on and off will be uncovered in a future essay.

Two: An awareness of who you are
It is essential to understand who you are and to do that, you need to recognize who you are not.
You are not your personality, ego, intellect, body, mind or thoughts. None are your true identity. You are a vibration-wave of intelligent energy that filters in, around, and out of the mind and body, you live with, in physical

form. We really should not give it a name, for if we call it soul, we will become mixed up in many intellectual/religious meanings, which have no meaning. However, for ease of language, we will refer to it as a soul.

A soul owns nothing and yet can manifest everything. If we live as a soul who is no-thing, we will have nothing to argue about. At the same time we will be aware we can manifest whatever our heart desires. If we try to manifest what our personalities desires, the results can be catastrophic. That is because our egos may possess other people's fallacious opinions, inaccurate beliefs and unsound dogmas, which we have taken to be true at an early stage in our development. Consequently, it has grown into our own reference points within our mind. In all likelihood, they did not originate from Gods mind.

Three: An awareness of why you exist
The reason you exist on earth in physical form is simple to know, hard to understand and seemingly impossible for most people to live. You exist to live in joy every moment on earth. This is the whole meaning behind the Kabbalah, every other holy book, wise doctrines and most religions in the world since humans could write words on paper.
Joy means:
J-ust
O-bey
Y-ourself
It is the authentic self that you just read in part two of this kit.

Four: The method to get inside the mind of God
Of course, it would be impossible to gain all the knowledge contained in the mind of the master creator/evolver who orchestrated the Cosmos. Nevertheless, we can obtain everything we need-to-know to live a life of true prosperity on earth. There is an abundance of everything we will ever desire, waiting for us, once we find our way inside Gods mind. Here is how we do it...

We just keep quite minded and stop our conscious minds, moaning and groaning ... We stop asking God for favors. We need to keep noiseless, soundless and in the complete empty silence of our subconscious mind. This will give our subconscious mind the opportunity to connect and communicate to the channels inside Gods mind. The soul is continually connected to the eternal source through a dimension we name spirit. That is why we can connect in less than a blink of the eye, once we comprehend how to communicate.

Five: Sourcing the intelligent wisdom outside time and space
Once we learn to silence our minds from all thoughts, we are able to
receive signals from a divine source of intelligence that is formless and
infinite. We can enter the kingdom of God by going inside our own
conscious mind, asking a question that requires an authentic answer, then
pass the question into our subconscious and allow the auto response
system that the creator invented, to function as it was made to do. Once we
can perfect empty silence for more that a few minutes we will find genuine
answers to our questions.

Our mind can transmit and receive signals in a form we term as thoughts.
Every thought we have is a sort of electric energy impulse that transmits
through and beyond space and time. It then reverberates back on earth and
can be accessed by all life forms that have a subconscious that is willing to
accept the message.
Depending on how that mind is programmed, it may or may not want to
interpret the message.

In the beginning of humanity, all thought originated from Gods mind in
pure form. However since humankind developed the intellectual part of the
brain, the thought process has become distorted and confused. Very few
people can still access pure thoughts direct from the source without any
taints or blemishes of past thinkers. The man-made-thoughts that are
tainted are referred to as The Devil. You see, they came from God
originally, but now humankind has distorted them and they have created
evil on earth.

If we want to live life without evil, all we have to do is recognize the
difference between the man-made artificial thoughts and those that
emanate from the mind of God. The fabricated stuff is mostly located in
the emotional part of our brain but that also contains the feelings of love
and joy that are not artificial. Most people live with a manufactured God,
which is opposed, by a supernatural devil. This is no more than a mirror
image of their own egos and personalities. Hence, it produces conflicts and
wars in their God's name. When we live outside the artificial world and
inside the mind of the creative intelligent energy that created the Cosmos,
we live within the original blueprints of creation.
You now have the teaching and learning of many hundreds of years of
studying the Kabbalah in a nutshell. What many people have studied for a
lifetime I have simplified in a few pages of text. You can read your
Kabbalah kit a few more times until you digest it and give your mind a few
weeks to chew it over within the subconscious. It will help you to continue

discovering all the magnificent beauty, virtue, grace and excellence your life on earth commands.

If the rich and famous are searching for methods to live a more authentic life then it must mean money and fame will not bring too much meaningful happiness. Therefore, you now have a choice in what you accept as your truths

As each day unfolds and the more you accept yourself as a bundle of authentic joy, the more love you will magnetize into your life. You will discover love and joy are not possessions; they are melded to one another in a sacred blessing of intelligent energy, which we can enact out in our authentic life on earth. You can now pack up your worries and anxieties in you kabbalah kit bag and smile...smile...smile

The Ambrosial Dream-keeper

Come, raise,
the divine goblet of joy,
be in celestial delight,
as mystic brightness
beams, from an eternal heart,
that cannot be observed,
by flesh and blood.
Choose wisdom's exquisite desire,
feast the loving souls enchantment,
pour forth the kindness cup of mortal service
Time cannot stop, its incessant gallop,
but the minds sacred dance, can slow down,
for awhile, to listen in celestial silence,
to the songs of spirits, melodic harmony.
The ambrosial dream-keeper,
sprinkles, sweet orchid fragrance,
on starlight serenades,
loves devotion constantly fills,
humanities empty vessels

The Finale Crescendo

Birth - Death and the Little Dash In-Between

It took a long time before you were born ... I mean a long, long, time. In fact, you could say it took an infinite amount of time before you were born, because your infinity was floating around before your birth. You now have a few years on earth before you will go back into infinity, with no physical presence on earth... at least, not in the mind and body you now rent for your present life-time. You are still in infinite mode right now, but with all the mortal distractions, not too many people are aware of their true identity.

"If we could see the miracle of a single flower clearly, our whole life would change." - Buddha.

Yes, we had a long time to think about what we wanted to do before we were born. We were given instructions on how to enjoy every moment ... How to soak up all the splendor earth provides. Also, just think about all of your ancestors and what they had to endure to survive the family line that leads to you. You do not have to be a historian to know about all the wars, famine, hardship, and difficulties that your past generations had to bare, before you popped out the womb.

"The learning and knowledge that we have, is, at the most, but little compared with that of which we are ignorant." - Plato.

Was it worth all the past turmoil and suffering to get you to your present destination? Do you feel grateful to your ancestors, or have you never bothered to thank them for their gift of life to you? Come to think about it, have they passed authentic information on to you, or has it been tainted with false be-lie-f systems?

"Dost thou love life? Then do not squander time, for that's the stuff life is made of." - Benjamin Franklin.

How are you doing regards following the cosmic script, written billions of years ago before time began?
Have you forgotten your original lines transmitted to all life forms from the fountain of universal wisdom?
Are you ad-libbing your role-plays and ignoring simple insights?
Are you making up new unfounded viewpoints without a happy purpose objective?

How quickly are you dashing ---- through you life right now?
Is your heart continually racing away at a fast beat?
Do you have no time to catch your breath?
Does each day seem to be a flash-in-the-pan, just like a flash of the camera?
Is your life a case of ... Birth-dash-Death - over - and - out...Is that all you want to embody before your lights go out?

"And in the end, it's not the years in your life that count. It's the life in your years." - Abraham Lincoln.

If not, then why not take the dash out of your life and your life will no longer be connected to your death ... What are the obsessions that dashes you to your death... Anger, fear, jealousy, hatred, and all negative emotions … Also, unhealthy foods, smoking, alcoholic drinks, pollution, lack of exercise,… all lead to a chronic disease laden death.

"Science is organized knowledge. Wisdom is organized life." - Immanuel Kant:

It not only dashes you towards ill health, it also depletes your wealth, because health-care does not come at a cheap price. Many people's bankruptcies are causes by payments to expensive medical establishments whose re-me-dies carry a hefty price tag. However, the good news is, most birth-dashes-to-death can be eliminated with the appropriate mind-set.

"And we should consider every day lost on which we have not danced at least once. And we should call every truth false which was not accompanied by at least one laugh." - Friedrich Nietzsche.

With no dashes to join you up to your demise, you will be free to live a healthy, prosperous life on earth and each second will be lived in a serene, tranquil paradise.
Taking the dash out of your life, will give you time to recall your cosmic script, written by the creator/evolver, who thought up your lines in the first place ... You can never replace originality with fake copies...sooner or later your mind and body realizes it has been deceived by an erroneous ego and hits back with disabling illness... The earlier you realize that fact- the sooner you will live more authentically in good health.

"A useless life is an early death." - Goethe.

There is no need to find newfangled ideas on how to enjoy your life, because, if you tune into each cell of your body and do the things that keep them happy ... health will be your reward.

The seconds will tick slower to the rhythmic celestial beat of the cosmic band and so will your heartbeat that is in tune with it.

Your breathing will be leisurely and measured and the only thing you will need to catch is your smile in the mirror.

You will no longer feel the need to march to the pulse of anyone else's unsound drumming.

"However mean your life is, meet it and live it: do not shun it and call it hard names. Cultivate poverty like a garden herb, like sage. Do not trouble yourself much to get new things, whether clothes or friends. Things do not change... we change. Sell your clothes and keep your thoughts." - Henry David Thoreau.

Your time on earth is just a spark in cosmic terms ... So, keep a smile on your face and enjoy every moment of your time on earth ...When you project true joy, you do a good deed for other people to copy. And when the time comes to depart to your eternal home ... you will be able to sit alongside the writer of your original script ... You will be able to chat like old friends because you will realize the authentic writer has been in your heart felt smile all the time you were on earth...

"The universe is transformation; our life is what our thoughts make it ... Remember that no man loses any other life than this which he now lives, nor lives any other than this which he now loses." - Marcus Aurelius.

If you feel the presence inside you now, as you read these words ... you are now sensing the great wisdom that all the wise sages have embraced ... You are now a polished pearl and nobody on earth will be able to wipe the smile from your kind, loving face... Life with no dashes sure make for a prosperous life of joyful vitality ... Treat every day as your miraculous birth-day and you will be treated to a miracle presence on earth that no money can buy ... who could ask for any-thing more!

A Merry Old Soul

I suppose you might say I look antiquated, but I don't feel it,

Strange is it not?

You would think I would be showing my age by now,
After all; I have been around for a lot longer than three million years.

What's that I hear you say
"How can that be?"
How can that not be, for I have nowhere to go.

Whilst it is true I persistently change my roles,
I still enjoy every one of them come what may.

On the surface,
 it could seem there is a lot of havoc and mayhem
 in my existence,
But it is just that; only on the surface.

Many of the characters I play appear to be enduring life,
Running around like headless chickens,
Taking things; Oh! so seriously,
Worries and anxieties abound.

Moreover, I sense it all and yet; I still love life's featured charades,
The make-believe world of deceits and lies,
My, my; ...what pretense. What grievous dis-ease of the mind.
I'm glad it is only fabricated illusions.

It fashions a variety show of drama, adventure, comedy
Not to mention sorrow,
"No! Please don't mention sorrow"...... I hear you cry,
Well, I did mention sorrow, for it all seems so real to the personalities I
play,
Good Game; Good Game.

You see; I have no need of pipe or fiddlers three,
For no matter what... I Am A Merry Old Soul,

For no matter what... No matter lasts,
Hee hee... Sorry but I have to chuckle,
For in reality... I will always wonder freely,

It looks like it's the end of another innings,
Pull up the wickets and change the rules then.

I presume I'll have a heavenly rest stop.
An episode of doing nothing in my true attire of vacuity,
It's all the same to me; it's all so sublimely divine,
What a great boss I have and no wages of sin.

I must slip into something a little more comfortable,
I guess it's time for a cup of spirituali-tea,
Bring on the elixir of life.

Be a dear and pass the honey.

^^^^^^^^^^^^^^^^^^^^^^^^^^^^^

Point of Life Web Site
http://www.pointoflife.com